Suzuki GT125 and GT185 Owners Workshop Manual

by Stewart W Wilkins

Models covered:

GT125L	First introduced into UK January 1974	
GT125M	First introduced into UK January 1975	123cc
GT125A	First introduced into UK October 1975	
GT185K	First introduced into UK May 1973	
GT185L	First introduced into UK January 1974	
GT185M	First introduced into UK January 1975	183cc
GT185A	First introduced into UK October 1975	

ISBN 085696 301 1

Printed in England

J H Haynes and Company Limited
Sparkford Yeovil Somerset England
distributed in the USA by
Haynes Publications Inc
9421 Winnetka Avenue
Chatsworth
California 91311 USA

Acknowledgements

Our grateful thanks are due to Heron Suzuki (GB) Ltd for their technical advice and permission to use their drawings.

We are also grateful to the Avon Rubber Company, who so kindly provided illustrations and advice about tyre fitting.

Brian Horsfall assisted with the stripdown and rebuild of the machine featured and devised methods to overcome the need for service tools. The photographic work that accompanies the text was arranged and taken by Les Brazier. Gratitude must also be extended to Jeff Clew who edited the text.

We are especially grateful to Nick Barnes of the Heron Suzuki Technical Service Department for checking the content of this manual and suggesting ways in which the text could be improved.

About this manual

The author of this manual has the conviction that the only way in which a meaningful and easy to follow text can be written is first to do the work himself, under conditions similar to those found in the average household. As a result, the hands seen in the photographs are those of the author. Even the machine photographed was not new; an example that had covered several thousand miles was selected so that the conditions encountered would be similar to those found by the average rider. Unless specially mentioned, and therefore considered essential, Suzuki service tools have not been used. There is invariably some alternative means of slackening or removing some vital component when service tools are not availabe and risk of damage has to be avoided at all costs.

Each of the six Chapters is divided into numbered Sections. Within the Sections are numbered paragraphs. In consequence, cross reference throughout this manual is both straightforward and logical. When a reference is made 'See Section 5.12' it means Section 5, paragraph 12 in the same Chapter. If another Chapter were meant, the text would read 'See Chapter 2, Section 5.12'. All photographs are captioned with a Section/paragraph number to which they refer and are always relevant to the Chapter text adjacent.

Figure numbers (usually line illustrations) appear in numerical order, within a given Chapter. Fig. 1.1 therefore refers to the first figure in Chapter 1. Left-hand and right-hand descriptions of the machines and their component parts refer to the right and left of a given machine when the rider is seated normally.

Whilst every care is taken to ensure that the information in this manual is correct no liability can be accepted by the authors or publishers for loss, damage or injury caused by any errors in or omissions from the information given.

The Suzuki GT 125 and GT 185 models

At the time of printing there has been three versions of the GT125 model and four of the GT185; the latest being the 'A' series. The changes have mostly been to the styling, although the twin leading shoe front brake of the GT185K model was replaced by an hydraulically-operated disc brake. The forks design has also been changed and there has been certain engine modifications.

The engine/gearbox unit of both the 125 and the 185 models bear a very close similarity to each other and utilise many of the same components. The machine actually stripped for the purpose of this manual was a GT125L model and, where differences occur between the two models, a note is made in the text, along with any alteration in procedure that may be required.

Contents

Note: General descriptions and specifications are given in each Chapter immediately after the list of Contents.
Fault diagnosis is given at the end of each appropriate Chapter.

SUZUKI GT125

SUZUKI GT185

Introduction to the Suzuki GT 125 and GT 185

The Suzuki GT125L was first introduced into the UK during January 1974. It followed the discontinuation of the T125-11 Stinger in April 1973. In December of the same year of introduction, the 'M' model was introduced. This model continued until along with some more changes, the 'A' model was introduced in October 1975. The GT185K was first introduced in this country in May 1973. In January 1974 the 'L' model was introduced, having an hydraulic front disc brake which replaced the twin leading front shoe brake fitted to the 'K' model. In October 1975 the 'M' model was introduced which was later superceded by the 'A' model in October 1975.

Dimensions, weights and capacities

The data given below relates to M and A models, unless otherwise stated.

	GT125		GT185	
	Imperial	Metric	Imperial	Metric
Overall length	75.2 in	1.910 m	78.0 in	1.980 m
Overall width	30.3 in	0.770 m	29.9 in	0.760 m
Overall height	41.9 in	1.065 m	39.8 in	1.010 m
Wheelbase	48.4 in	1.230 m	50.6 in	1.285 m
Ground clearance	5.5 in	0.140 m	6.5 in	0.165 m
Dry weight	238 lb	108 kg	253 lb	115 kg
Fuel tank, total	2.2 gal	10 litres	2.2 gal	10 litres
reserve	3.5 pt	2 litres	3.5 pt	2 litres
Oil tank capacity (engine)	2.1 pt	1.2 litres	2.1 pt	1.2 litres
Gearbox capacity	1.4 pt	800 cc	1.4 pt	800 cc
Front fork leg (each)	4.4 oz	125 cc	4.4 oz	125 cc (K models) 130 cc (L, M and A models)

Ordering spare parts

When ordering spare parts for any Suzuki, it is advisable to deal direct with an official Suzuki dealer who should be able to supply most of the parts ex stock. Parts cannot be obtained from Suzuki direct and all orders must be routed via an approved dealer even if the parts required are not held in stock. Always quote the engine and frame numbers in full, especially if parts are required for earlier models.

The engine number is stamped on the upper rear of the crankcase, on the left-hand side.

The frame number is stamped along the right-hand side of the steering head. There is also a manufacturers' nameplate rivetted to the left-hand side of the steering head, on which the corresponding frame and engine numbers are stamped.

Always fit parts of genuine Suzuki manufacture and not pattern parts, which are often available at lower cost. Pattern parts do not necessarily make a satisfactory replacement for the originals and there are many cases where reduced life or sudden failure has occurred, to the detriment of performance.

Some of the more expendable parts such as spark plugs, bulbs, tyres, oils and greases etc., can be obtained from accessory shops and motor factors, who have convenient opening hours, charge lower prices and can often be found not far from home. It is also possible to obtain parts on a Mail Order basis from a number of specialists who advertise regularly in the motor cycle magazines.

Engine number location

Frame number location

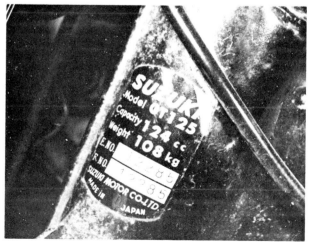

Manufacturer's nameplate which gives details of the machine

Routine maintenance

Periodic routine maintenance is a continuous process that commences immediately the machine is used and continues until the machine is no longer fit for use. It must be carried out at specific mileage recordings, or on a calendar basis if the machine is not used regularly, whichever is the soonest. Maintenance should be regarded as an insurance policy, to help keep the machine in the peak of condition and to ensure long, trouble-free use. It has the additional benefit of giving early warning of any faults that may develop and will act as a safety check, to the obvious advantage of both rider and machine alike.

The various maintenance tasks are described under their respective mileage and calendar headings. Accompanying diagrams are provided, where necessary. It should be remembered that the interval between the various maintenance tasks serves only as a guide. As the machine gets older, is driven hard or is used under particularly adverse conditions, it is advisable to reduce the interval between each check.

If a specific item is mentioned but not described in detail, it will be covered fully in the appropriate chapter. No special tools are required for the normal routine maintenance tasks. Those contained in the tool kit supplied with every new machine will suffice, but if they are not available, the tools found in the average household will make an adequate substitute.

Weekly or every 200 miles

Check the oil level through the inspection window in the oil tank. If the level is low, it must be topped-up with a recommended two-stroke oil.

Check the adjustment of the rear brake and the fluid level in the front brake reservoir.

Adjust the play in the rear chain, if necessary.

Check the tyre pressures. Always check the tyres when they are cold, as hot tyres will give a high pressure reading.

Check the level of the electrolyte in the battery. Use only distilled water to top-up, unless there has been a spillage of acid, when electrolyte of the correct specific gravity should be used to replenish the battery.

Oil all exposed control cables and joints.

Check the gearbox oil level and replenish, if necessary.

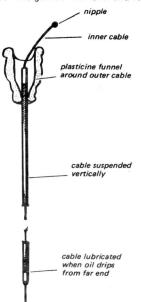

nipple

inner cable

plasticine funnel around outer cable

cable suspended vertically

cable lubricated when oil drips from far end

Fig. RM1. Oiling the control cables

Three monthly or every 2000 miles

Complete all the checks under the weekly heading and carry out the following:

Check the exhaust pipe joints for tightness.

Lubricate the felt contact breaker cam oiler.

Check the front disc pad for wear.

Remove and clean the air cleaner.

Clean and reset the spark plug gaps.

Clean the petrol tap filters.

Adjust the play in the control cables and rods.

Adjust the carburettor if necessary, to obtain a smooth tickover.

Check the contact breaker gaps and the ignition timing.

Check the cylinder head nuts and re-tighten if necessary.

Check for play in the steering head bearings and adjust, if necessary.

Check the wheel spokes for tightness or breakage.

Check the clutch adjustment.

Lubricate the rear chain.

Change the transmission oil.

Check the oil pump cable adjustment.

Six monthly or every 4000 miles

Complete all the checks under the previous headings and then as follows:

Renew the spark plugs.

Grease the throttle twist grip.

Check the tightness of all the nuts and bolts.

Remove wheels. Check and clean brake shoes etc. as described in Chapter 5.7 or 5.14.

Yearly or every 6000 miles

Complete all the checks under the previous headings and then as follows:

Dismantle, clean and examine the carburettors.

Renew the contact breaker assemblies.

Remove both wheels, regrease the bearings and brake operating cams. Check also the brake linings for wear.

Check and regrease the steering head bearings.

Check the level of the battery electrolyte

Check the level of the brake fluid and ...

... top up if necessary

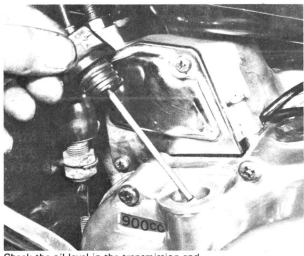

Check the oil level in the transmission and ...

... top up if necessary

Do not let the oil tank run dry

A spray lubricant can be used on the rear chain

Summary of routine maintenance settings and capacities

All the settings and capacities are the same for both the GT125 and GT185 models.

	GT125	GT185
Spark plug	NGK B8HS	NGK B8HS
	Imperial	**Metric**
Spark plug gap	0.024 - 0.028 in	0.6 - 0.7 mm
Contact breaker points gap	0.012 - 0.016 in	0.3 - 0.4 mm
Gearbox capacity	1.4 pt	800 cc 900 cc (GT125L models)
Front fork leg capacity (each leg)	4.6 oz	125 cc (K models) 130 cc (L, M and A models)
Tyre pressure, front	25 psi	1.75 kg/sq cm
rear (solo)	28 psi	2.0 kg/sq cm
rear (passenger)	32 psi	2.25 kg/sq cm

Recommended lubricants and fluids

Component	Grade	Description
Engine oil (oil tank)	SAE 30	... Non diluent two-stroke oil
Gearbox/transmission oil	SAE 20W/50	⎫
Front forks	SAE 10W/30	⎬ Automatic Transmission Fluid
Final drive chain		... ... Heavyweight motor oil or proprietary chain lubricant
Control cables		... ... Light oil
All greasing points		... ... Proprietary lithium base grease

For specific lubricant recommendations apply to Heron Suzuki GB Limited Technical Department.

Tightening torques

	lb/ft	kg/cm
Engine bolts 8 mm	9.5 - 17	130 - 230
10 mm	18 - 29	250 - 400
Cylinder head	14 - 18	200 - 250
Rotor or dynamo/starter bolt	6.6 - 10	90 - 140
Oil pump and cover bolts	1.5 - 2.9	20 - 40
Clutch centre nut	14 - 22	200 - 300
Crankcase 6 mm	4.4 - 7.3	60 - 100
8 mm	9.5 - 17	130 - 230
Gear lever pinch bolt	4.4 - 7.3	60 - 100
Kickstart pinch bolt	18 - 29	250 - 400
Swining arm pivot nut	22 - 32	300 - 450
Front wheel spindle nut	26 - 38	360 - 520
Master cylinder clamp bolt	4 - 6	50 - 80
Hydraulic union bolt	11 - 18	150 - 250
Brake pipe nut	10 - 13	130 - 180
Caliper bolt	18 - 29	250 - 400
Brake hose joint	18 - 25	250 - 350
Bleed nipple	4 - 7	60 - 90
Handlebar clamp bolt	9 - 14	120 - 200
Top yoke pinch bolt	14 - 22	200 - 300
Bottom yoke pinch bolt	18 - 25	250 - 350
Steering column bolt	25 - 40	350 - 550
Rear suspension unit nuts	14 - 22	200 - 300
Rear brake torque arm	7 - 11	100 - 150
Rear wheel spindle nut	26 - 28	360 - 520
Sprocket carrier nut	40 - 51	550 - 700

Chapter 1 Engine, clutch and gearbox

Contents

Specifications

Engine

	GT125	GT185
Type	Two cycle, air cooled, twin cylinder	
Capacity	124 cc (7.5 cu in)	184 cc (11.2 cu in)
Bore	43 mm (1.69 in)	49 mm (1.93 in)
Stroke	43 mm (1.69 in)	49 mm (1.93 in)
Corrected compression ratio	6.8 : 1	7 : 1
Maximum hp	16 @ 9500 rpm	20 @ 7500 rpm (L, M and A models)
Maximum torque	1.30 kg m (9.40 ft lb) @ 9000 rpm	14.7 ft lb @ 6000 rpm (L, M and A models)
Starter	Kick	Electric and kick

Clutch

	GT125	GT185
Type	Wet, multiplate	
Nos. friction plates	5	6
Nos. plain plates	4	5
Primary drive		
Type	Helical gear, with tensioned quitening gear	Helical gear
Reduction	61T/19T (3.210) (L and M models) 47/14 (A models)	61T/19T (3.210)

Gearbox

Type	...	...	...	...	...	...	...	...	...	All indirect, five-speed, drum type selector
Ratios										
1st	...	...	...	...	...	...	...	...	...	33T/11T (3.000) 33T/12T (2.750)
2nd	...	...	...	...	...	...	...	...	...	29T/16T (1.812) 29T/16T (1.812)
3rd	...	...	...	...	...	...	...	...	...	25T/20T (1.250) 25T/20T (1.250)
4th	...	...	...	...	...	...	...	...	...	22T/23T (0.956) L & M models 23T/23T (1.000)
										23T/23T (1.000) A models
5th	...	...	...	...	...	...	...	...	...	20T/25T (0800) L & M models 20T/25T (0.800)
										21T/24T A models

1 General description

The Suzuki GT125 and GT185 models are both fitted with air cooled twin cylinder two-stroke engines. Engine lubrication is provided by the Suzuki C.C.1 system. Transmission is by helical gear to a wet multiplate clutch, which drives a five-speed gearbox.

2 Operations with the engine/gearbox in frame

It is not necessary to remove the engine/gearbox unit from the frame unless the crankshaft assembly and/or the gearbox components need attention. Most operations can be accomplished with the engine in place, such as:

1 Removal and replacement of the cylinder head.
2 Removal and replacement of the cylinder barrels and pistons.
3 Removal and replacement of the flywheel alternator or dynamo contact breaker assembly.
4 Removal and replacement of the clutch
5 Removal and replacement of the kickstart return spring.

When several operations need to be undertaken at the same time, it would probably be advantageous to remove the complete unit from the frame, a comparatively simple operation that can take as little as thirty minutes. This will afford better access and more working space.

3 Engine/gearbox - removal from frame

1 Remove the right-hand side panel and disconnect the battery at the connector.
2 Remove both the gearbox and kickstart lever bolts and pull the levers off their shafts.
3 Turn off the petrol tap and disconnect the petrol pipe. Lift the seat and unhook the petrol tank. Remove it by lifting it up and back.
4 Slacken the air filter hose clips and pull the hoses off the carburettors. Unscrew the carburettor tops and carefully lift out the throttle slides. Label the slides so that they will be replaced in the same carburettor. Hang the slides out of the way.
5 The carburettors can now be removed by either slackening the hose clips or the carburettor clip bolts, depending on the model.
6 Remove the oil pump inspection cover and unclip the throttle control cable. Free the cable by unscrewing it from the oil pump cover.
7 Disconnect the clutch cable at the handlebar lever and pull it clear.
8 Remove the spark plug caps.
10 Disconnect the wires from the alternator or dynamo/starter at the cable junction and pull the wires clear. On the GT185 model only, remove the engine earth wire.
11 Disconnect the chain at its spring link and pull it clear.
12 Remove the exhaust pipes by undoing the two bolts on each cylinder. Remove the exhaust/silencer from the swinging arm pivot bolt (GT125) or the pillion footrests (GT185).
13 Remove the banjo bolt oil feed pipe at the oil pump end and either drain the tank or hook up the pipe and block the end, to prevent the oil from being spilled.

14 The engine is held in the frame by engine plates and six bolts on the GT125 and five on the GT185. Support the engine on wooden blocks. Remove the bolts and lift the engine up and out of the right-hand side of the frame.

4 Dismantling the engine, clutch and gearbox - general

Before commencing work on the engine unit, the external surfaces should be cleaned thoroughly. A motor cycle engine has very little protection from road grit and other foreign matter, which will find its way into the dismantled engine if this simple precaution is not observed. One of the proprietary cleaning compounds such as 'Gunk' can be used to good effect, particularly if the compound is allowed to work into the film of oil and grease before it is washed away. When washing down, make sure that water cannot enter the carburettor or the electrical system, particularly if these parts have been exposed.

Never use undue force to remove any stubborn parts, unless mention is made of this requirement. There is invariably good reason why a part is difficult to remove, often because the dismantling operation has been tackled in the wrong sequence. Dismantling will be made easier if a simple engine stand is constructed that will correspond with the engine mounting points. This arrangement will permit the complete unit to be clamped rigidly to the workbench, leaving both hands free.

5 Preventing the engine from turning both for dismantling and reassembly purposes

1 It is often necessary to stop the engine from rotating so that a component can be removed or tightened eg; engine sprocket nut or clutch centre nut. One way of achieving this that can be used during dismantling and reassembly is by placing a round metal bar through the small end boss and resting this bar on two pieces of wood placed on top of the crankcase mouth. On no account must the metal bar be allowed to bear directly down onto the gasket face of the crankcase mouth, otherwsie damage will occur and cause a loss of primary compression.

6 Cylinder head and cover - removal

1 Unscrew the four crosshead screws that retain the cylinder head cover. Note the washers and sleeve fitted in the rubber grommets. Lift off the cover.
2 Remove the spark plugs.
3 To prevent distortion, slacken off the cylinder head nuts in a diagonal sequence. Remove the nuts and washers and lift off the cylinder head. Remove the head gasket.

7 Cylinder block - removal

1 Lift off each cylinder barrel separately whilst supporting the connecting rods and pistons. Stuff the crankcase mouth with rag to protect the edges and also to prevent anything being dropped down into the engine. If a barrel is stuck, gently tap around the joint with a soft faced hammer.
2 On GT185 models, the cylinder barrels are held by four nuts around the flange, which must be removed before each barrel can be lifted off.

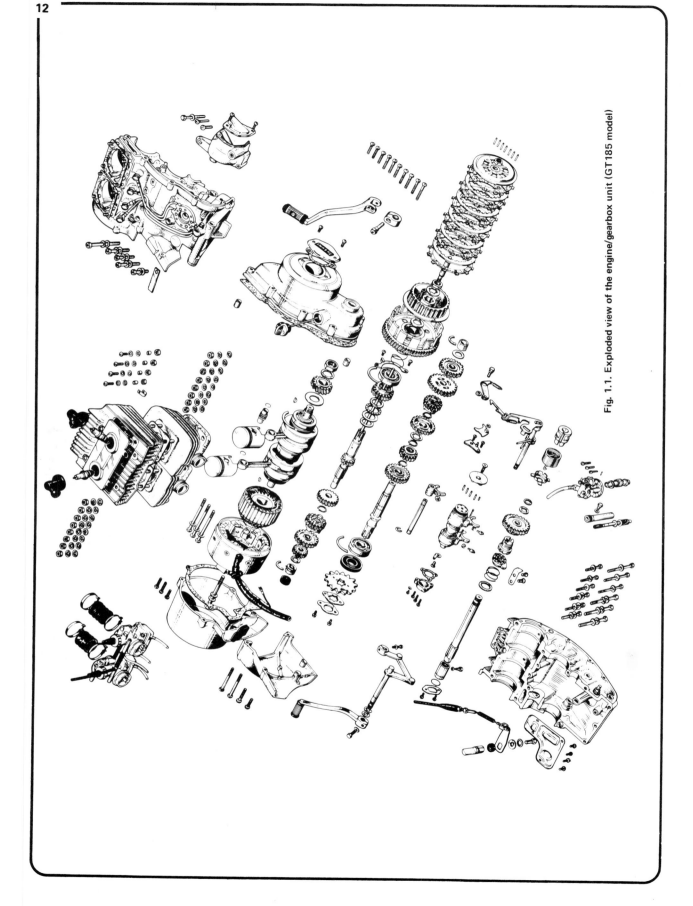

Fig. 1.1. Exploded view of the engine/gearbox unit (GT185 model)

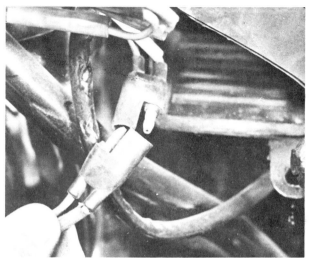

3.1 Disconnect the battery at the junction connector

3.4 Remove the throttle slides, taking care not to bend needles

3.7 Unhook the oil pump cable from the pump arm

3.11 Remove the chain at its spring link

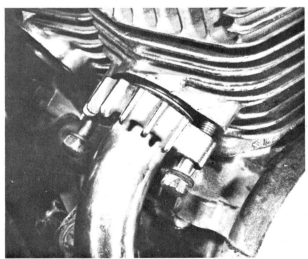

3.12a Remove the exhaust pipe clamp bolts and ...

3.12b ... the nut on the swinging arm pivot

3.14a Remove the front engine plate bolts ...

3.14b ... the lower engine bolt and ...

3.14c ... the rearmost bolt

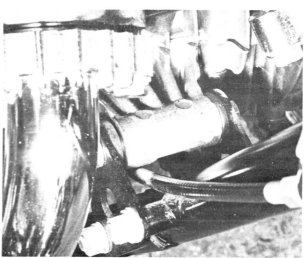
3.14d The GT185 is mounted in rubber bushes.

5.1 Method used to prevent engine from rotating. Note the wooden batterns.

6.3 Lift off the cylinder head

7.2 The GT185 model has cylinder base nuts

8 Pistons and small end - removal

1 Remove both the piston circlips from each piston and discard them. They should never be reused.
2 Push out the gudgeon pins from the pistons. If they are a tight fit, warm the pistons with some rag that has been soaked in boiling water, and wrung out.
3 The needle roller small end bearings are a sliding fit in the boss of each connecting rod and will push out of position. Each piston and its associated components must be replaced in its original position. Therefore keep the parts separate and preferably mark them.

9 Oil pump and cover - removal

1 Remove the oil pump cover by undoing the three crosshead screws (or two screws and one bolt).
2 Remove the three crosshead screws securing the oil pump and lift the pump off its distribution manifold. Be careful that the oil pump drive pin does not fall out of the drive shaft and get lost.
3 Remove the four rubber 'O'-rings from the oil manifold and undo the four banjo bolts in the crankcase. A plastic washer is placed either side of the banjos. The oil manifold can now be lifted clear.

10 Alternator or dynamo/starter and cover - removal

1 Remove the three alternator cover crosshead screws and lift the cover off.
2 Unscrew the three crosshead screws that retain the stator or field coils and lift the assembly off, complete with the contact breaker plate.
3 Lock the engine as described earlier and remove the rotor bolt. Lift off the cam, where it is separated. Use either the Suzuki service tool or a three jaw puller to remove the rotor. A puller may damage the armature fitted to the GT185, thus for this model the Suzuki service tool must be used. If this is not available, a use of a short rod (an old bolt with the head cut off) and insert this into the hole left by the armature bolt. Then screw in a suitable bolt, to act as an extractor. If, with some pressure on the bolt, the armature has still not extracted, hit the end of the bolt sharply with a hammer. This should shock it off the taper.

11 Gear lever linkage - removal

1 Mark the gear linkage arm and shaft with a centre punch, so that they can be replaced in the same positions, during reassembly.
2 Undo and remove the clamp bolt. Pull off the linkage.

12 Neutral light switch - removal

1 Undo and remove the three crosshead retaining screws and lift off the switch.
2 Remove the central crosshead screw and lift off the contact.

13 Final drive sprocket - removal

1 Undo the two bolts, rotate the lockwasher and lift it off. Lift off the sprocket.

14 Clutch operating mechanism - removal

GT125 model
1 The clutch operating mechanism is contained within the sprocket cover and consists of a lever connected to a worm, which in turn, applies pressure to the pushrod which lifts the clutch.
2 Access to the mechanism is obtained by removing the clutch adjuster rear cover. The mechanism should require little attention, except for the occasional greasing.
3 Remove the sprocket cover complete with the mechanism when dismantling the engine.
4 Clutch adjustment is described in Section 51 of this Chapter.

GT185 model
5 The clutch operating mechanism is located underneath the engine. It operates on a simple cam principle, adjustment being carried out by a screw in the pressure plate.
6 The mechanism is retained by a bolt, which should be removed, allowing the cam to be withdrawn.
7 Check the condition of the seal and renew as necessary.
8 Remove the mechanism when dismantling the engine.
9 Clutch adjustment is described in Section 51 of this Chapter.

15 Primary drive cover - removal

1 Remove the crosshead screws and lift the cover off. Remove the gasket, if it is not attached to the cover.

16 Kickstart return spring - removal

1 Remove the large washer and slide out the plastic sleeve. Unhook the spring and remove it from the kickstart shaft. There is a shaped spacer fitted behind the spring, which must also be removed.

17 Clutch and primary drive - removal

1 Removal of the clutch pressure plate can prove a little difficult since the clutch springs have to be pulled out to free their holding pins. Use a pair of circlip pliers or a hooked piece of stout wire to pull out the spring and enable the pin to be removed. Be careful not to drop the pin into the engine, where it could fall into the gearbox.
2 After removing the pins, lift off the pressure plate, followed by the drive and driven plates. On the GT125 model, also remove the clutch mushroom.

3   Lock the engine as described earlier. Bend down the tab on the clutch centre lockwasher and remove the nut. Lift out the clutch centre and thrust washer(s).
4   Pull the clutch housing off the shaft. This can be a little difficult on the GT125 and GT185 models since it is held in position by a spring clip at the rear. Remove the clutch sleeve and on the GT185K, L and M models, the spring.
5   Knock down the tab on the lockwasher of the primary drive gear and undo the nut. Pull the gear off the crankshaft (parallel shaft). Remove the Woodruff key and spacing washer. On the GT125 model, the primary drive gear consists of two gears spring loaded against each other, to reduce transmission noise.

18 Gear selector mechanism - removal

1   Remove the crosshead countersunk screw that retains the pin plate.
2   Remove the shouldered bolt and washer from the positive stop lever. Remove the lever by unhooking its spring from the bearing retainer.

3   Lift off the selector pawl (after removing the E-clip, where fitted). Temporarily replace the pin plate and screw.
4   Unhook the gear lever shaft and linkage. Withdraw it from the crankcase.
5   Remove the two countersunk crosshead screws from the guide plate and remove the plate.
6   Remove the bearing retainer plate by undoing the two crosshead screws.

19 Separating the crankcases

1   Remove the seventeen crankcase bolts; two on the top and fifteen underneath. Each bolt has a number stamped by it. Start at the highest number (seventeen) and work down.
2   Part the crankcases by inverting them and lifting off the bottom half, leaving all the components in the top. If the halves are tight, use a soft faced hammer to jar them apart. On no account use a screwdriver to lever them apart since it will inevitably damage the gasket faces. If the crankcases will not part, check that all the bolts have been removed.

8.2 Push out the gudgeon pin, after removing circlips

9.2 Lift off the oil pump. Note 'O' rings

9.3 Remove the oil manifold and feed pipes

10.2a The alternator is held by three screws

10.2b Lift off the stator assembly

10.3a Remove the centre bolt and cam (where applicable)

10.3b A universal puller is used to remove the rotor (GT125 models)

12.2 A cross-head screw retains the neutral wiper contact

14.1 The clutch operating mechanism is inside cover

16.1 Slide off the plastic sleeve

17.1 A pair of pliers can be used to pull out spring retainers

17.2 Lift out all the clutch plates

17.3 Remove the clutch centre. Note the thrust washers behind

17.5 The primary drive gear fits onto a parallel keyed shaft

18.1 Remove the pin retaining plate

18.4 Unhook and lift out the gear lever shaft

18.6 Remove the bearing retaining plate

20 Crankshaft and gears - removal

1 Note the position of all the bearing and oil seal retaining clips and then remove them.
2 Lift out the complete crankshaft assembly and place it on one side.
3 Lift out both the input and output shafts, complete with their gears.

21 Tachometer and oil pump drives - removal

1 Remove the bolt from the tachometer stem on the crankcase. Pull out the sleeve and tachometer drive shaft. Note that there is a rubber 'O'-ring fitted to the sleeve and a thrust washer between the sleeve and shaft.
2 Lift out the oil pump drive shaft.

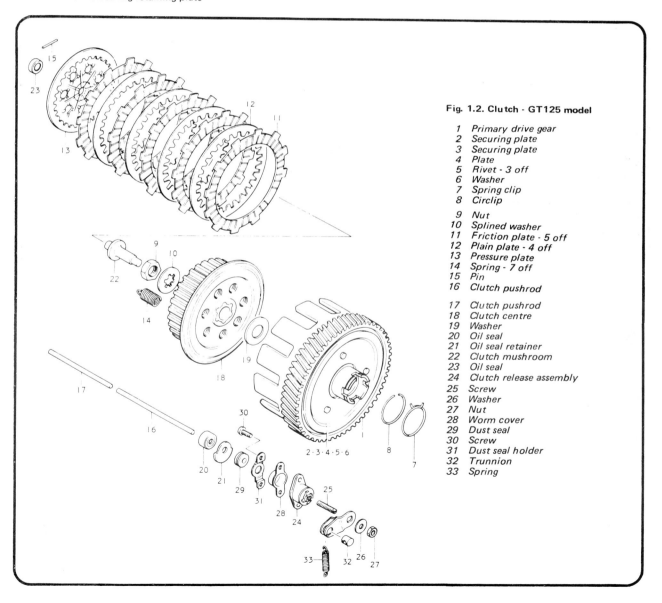

Fig. 1.2. Clutch - GT125 model

1 Primary drive gear
2 Securing plate
3 Securing plate
4 Plate
5 Rivet - 3 off
6 Washer
7 Spring clip
8 Circlip

9 Nut
10 Splined washer
11 Friction plate - 5 off
12 Plain plate - 4 off
13 Pressure plate
14 Spring - 7 off
15 Pin
16 Clutch pushrod

17 Clutch pushrod
18 Clutch centre
19 Washer
20 Oil seal
21 Oil seal retainer
22 Clutch mushroom
23 Oil seal
24 Clutch release assembly
25 Screw
26 Washer
27 Nut
28 Worm cover
29 Dust seal
30 Screw
31 Dust seal holder
32 Trunnion
33 Spring

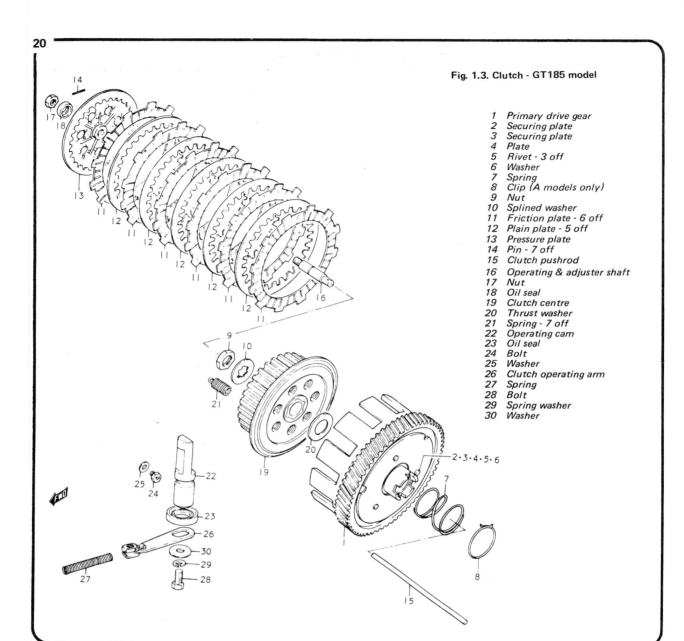

Fig. 1.3. Clutch - GT185 model

1 Primary drive gear
2 Securing plate
3 Securing plate
4 Plate
5 Rivet - 3 off
6 Washer
7 Spring
8 Clip (A models only)
9 Nut
10 Splined washer
11 Friction plate - 6 off
12 Plain plate - 5 off
13 Pressure plate
14 Pin - 7 off
15 Clutch pushrod
16 Operating & adjuster shaft
17 Nut
18 Oil seal
19 Clutch centre
20 Thrust washer
21 Spring - 7 off
22 Operating cam
23 Oil seal
24 Bolt
25 Washer
26 Clutch operating arm
27 Spring
28 Bolt
29 Spring washer
30 Washer

20.1 The complete gear cluster assembly

21.1 Pull out the tachometer drive shaft

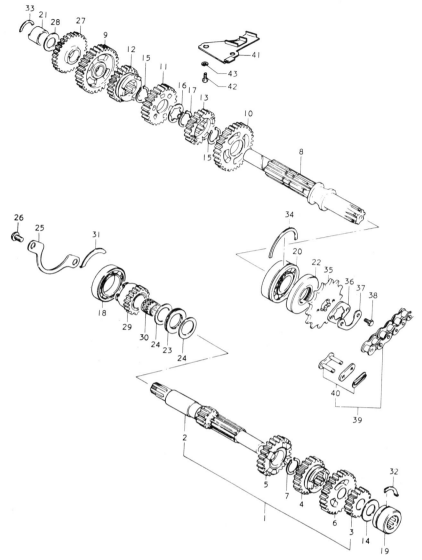

Fig. 1.4. Gearbox components

1   *Input shaft and gears complete*
2   *Input shaft - 11T*
3   *2nd drive gear - 16T*
4   *3rd drive gear - 20T*
5   *4th drive gear - 23T*
6   *5th drive gear - 24 or 25T*
7   *Circlip*
8   *Output shaft*
9   *1st driven gear - 33T*
10 *2nd driven gear - 29T*
11 *3rd driven gear - 25T*
12 *4th driven gear - 22 or 23T*
13 *5th driven gear - 20 or 21T*
14 *Washer*
15 *Circlip - 2 off*
16 *Splined washer*
17 *Circlip*
18 *Bearing*
19 *Bearing*
20 *Bearing*
21 *Bush*
22 *Oil seal*
23 *Bearing*
24 *Washer - 2 off*
25 *Bearing retainer*
26 *Screw - 2 off*
27 *Kickstart idler gear*
28 *Spring washer*
29 *Kickstarter drive gear*
30 *Bearing*
31 *Bearing retainer clip*
32 *Bearing retainer clip*
33 *Bearing retainer clip*
34 *Bearing retainer clip*
35 *Final drive sprocket - 13 or 14T*
36 *Retainer plate*
37 *Lock washer*
38 *Bolt - 2 off*
39 *Final drive chain*
40 *Spring link*
41 *Oil deflector plate*
42 *Screw - 2 off*
43 *Spring washer*

22 Kickstart mechanism and gear selectors - removal

1   Remove the two crosshead screws on the left-hand end of the kickstart shaft. Lift off the retaining plate and pull out the square headed sleeve. Note that the sleeve is fitted with a 'O'-ring seal.

2   The kickstart shaft can now be removed, by pulling it out from the sleeve end. Note the order of the components as they come off the shaft.

3   Remove the countersunk crosshead screw on the left-hand end of the selector drum and lift off the neutral light switch wiper contact (if this has not already been done).

4   Remove the split pin in each of the selector forks and lift out the guide pin and roller.

5   The selector drum can now be removed by pulling it out from the right-hand side.

6   The third selector fork is freed by removing the two E-clips from the shaft and then by pulling it out from the right-hand side.

7   Unhook the neutral cam arm and spring from the oil baffle plate and remove them.

8   There is no necessity to remove either the oil baffle plate or the kickstart guide from the crankcase. If, through damage, either has to be removed, they are both retained by two crosshead screws.

23 Examination and renovation - general

1   Before examining the component parts of the dismantled engine/gear unit for wear, it is essential that they should be cleaned thoroughly. Use a paraffin/petrol mix to remove all traces of oil and sludge which may have accumulated within the engine.

2   Examine the crankcase castings for cracks or other signs of damage. If a crack is discovered, it will require professional attention, or in an extreme case, renewal of the casting.

3   Examine carefully each part to determine the extent of wear. If in doubt, check with the tolerance figures whenever they are quoted in the text. The following Sections will indicate what type of wear can be expected and in many cases, the acceptable limits.

4   Use clean, lint-free rags for cleaning and drying the various components, otherwise there is risk of small particles obstructing the internal oilways.

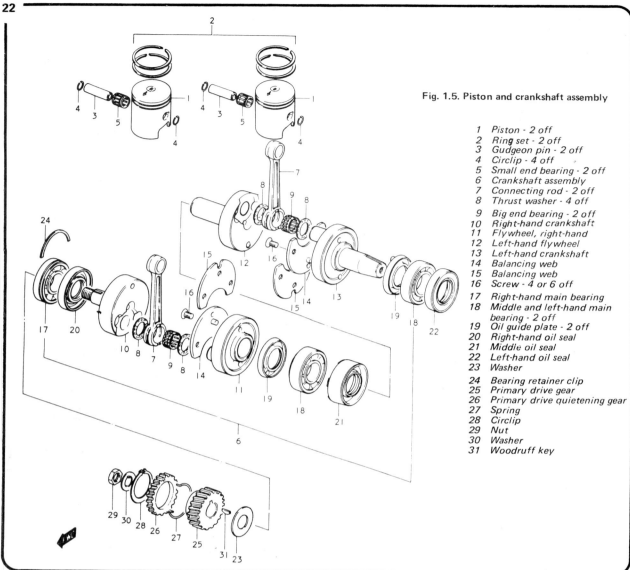

Fig. 1.5. Piston and crankshaft assembly

1	Piston - 2 off
2	Ring set - 2 off
3	Gudgeon pin - 2 off
4	Circlip - 4 off
5	Small end bearing - 2 off
6	Crankshaft assembly
7	Connecting rod - 2 off
8	Thrust washer - 4 off
9	Big end bearing - 2 off
10	Right-hand crankshaft
11	Flywheel, right-hand
12	Left-hand flywheel
13	Left-hand crankshaft
14	Balancing web
15	Balancing web
16	Screw - 4 or 6 off
17	Right-hand main bearing
18	Middle and left-hand main bearing - 2 off
19	Oil guide plate - 2 off
20	Right-hand oil seal
21	Middle oil seal
22	Left-hand oil seal
23	Washer
24	Bearing retainer clip
25	Primary drive gear
26	Primary drive quietening gear
27	Spring
28	Circlip
29	Nut
30	Washer
31	Woodruff key

22.1 Note the O-ring seal on the sleeve

22.2 Pull out the kickstart shaft

22.5 Slide the selector drum out

22.6 Pull out the remaining selector shaft

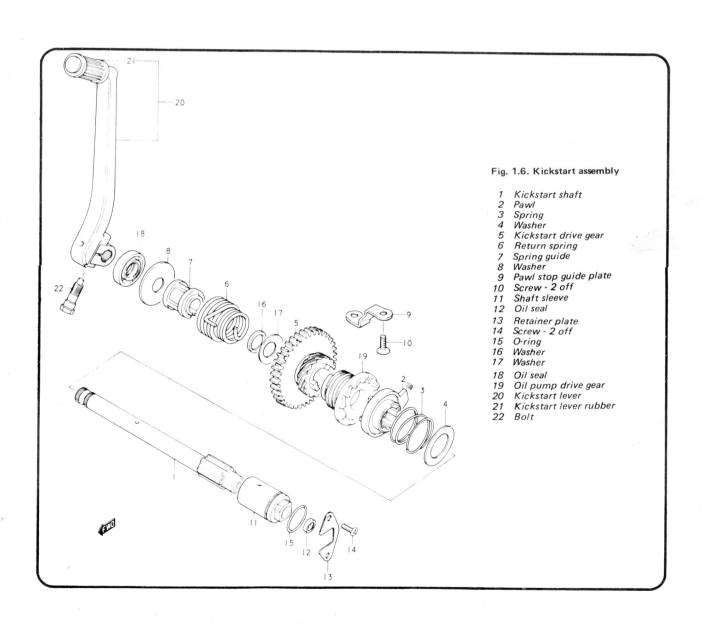

Fig. 1.6. Kickstart assembly

1 Kickstart shaft
2 Pawl
3 Spring
4 Washer
5 Kickstart drive gear
6 Return spring
7 Spring guide
8 Washer
9 Pawl stop guide plate
10 Screw - 2 off
11 Shaft sleeve
12 Oil seal
13 Retainer plate
14 Screw - 2 off
15 O-ring
16 Washer
17 Washer
18 Oil seal
19 Oil pump drive gear
20 Kickstart lever
21 Kickstart lever rubber
22 Bolt

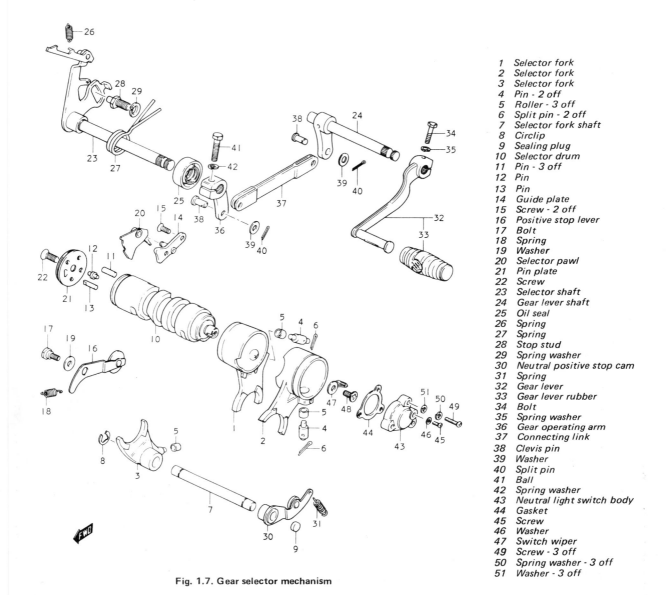

1	Selector fork
2	Selector fork
3	Selector fork
4	Pin - 2 off
5	Roller - 3 off
6	Split pin - 2 off
7	Selector fork shaft
8	Circlip
9	Sealing plug
10	Selector drum
11	Pin - 3 off
12	Pin
13	Pin
14	Guide plate
15	Screw - 2 off
16	Positive stop lever
17	Bolt
18	Spring
19	Washer
20	Selector pawl
21	Pin plate
22	Screw
23	Selector shaft
24	Gear lever shaft
25	Oil seal
26	Spring
27	Spring
28	Stop stud
29	Spring washer
30	Neutral positive stop cam
31	Spring
32	Gear lever
33	Gear lever rubber
34	Bolt
35	Spring washer
36	Gear operating arm
37	Connecting link
38	Clevis pin
39	Washer
40	Split pin
41	Ball
42	Spring washer
43	Neutral light switch body
44	Gasket
45	Screw
46	Washer
47	Switch wiper
49	Screw - 3 off
50	Spring washer - 3 off
51	Washer - 3 off

Fig. 1.7. Gear selector mechanism

24 Decarbonising

1   Remove any build-up of carbon on each piston and/or cylinder head, using wire wool and oil. Any obstinate carbon deposits should be scraped off with a soft metal (aluminium) scraper so as to prevent damage to the head or piston. Do not forget to clean the ports in the cylinder block.

2   There will possibly be a ridge of carbon at the top of each cylinder barrel; it is imperative to remove this is new pistons and/or rings are to be fitted.

25 Cylinder head - examination and renovation

1   Clean out any mud and dirt from the fins to prevent overheating.

2   Check the condition of the thread in each spark plug hole. If it is damaged, an effective repair can be made by using a Helicoil thread insert. This service is available from most Suzuki agents. The cause of a damaged thread can usually be traced to over tightening of the plug or using a plug of too long a reach. Always use the correct plug and do not overtighten (approximately 2.5 kg m or 18 lb ft as a maximum).

3   Check the cylinder head for warpage (usually caused by uneven tightening and/or over-tightening), with a straight edge across several places on the gasket 'ace; or preferably, with engineer's blue on a surface plate (a sheet of plate glass can be used as a substitute for a surface plate). If the cylinder head is warped, grind it down on a surface plate with emery paper. Start with 200 grade paper and finish with 400 grade and oil.

4   If it is necessary to remove a substantial amount of metal before the cylinder head will seat correctly, a new cylinder head should be obtained.

26 Pistons and rings - examination and renovation

1   Remove the piston rings by expanding them carefully with the thumbs and lifting the opposite side off the piston. Keep the rings separate so that they can be replaced in the same groove.
2   The two rings are of the Keystone type ie; tapering inwards on the top surface (see Fig. 1.8), on the GT185 model whilst only the top ring is of the Keystone type on the GT125 model, the second ring being plain. This type of ring is used to help prevent the build-up of carbon and sticking rings, which is a common malaise of two-strokes.
3   Check the piston rings by placing each ring in the bottom of the bore (this is the least worn part of the bore). Press down a little way with the piston to make sure that it is square in the bore. Measure the end gap and compare with the wear limit. Renew if necessary.
4   When fitting new rings always check the end gap and enlarge it, if necessary, by filing with a needle file.
5   Check that each piston and bore is not scored, particularly if the engine has tightened up or seized. If the bore is badly scored, it will require a rebore and oversize piston. If the scoring is not too severe or the piston has just picked up, it is possible to remove the high spots by careful use of a needle file. Do not try to remove the file marks completely, since they will act as oil pockets and assist during the initial bedding in.
6   Before replacing the rings on the piston, make sure that the ring lands are clear of carbon. Be very careful not to damage the lands when cleaning. Also, check that the ring locating pegs are not worn. (If they are, a new piston will have to be obtained).
7   The rings will have worn to the shape of the bore in use (and are different types on the GT125 model), and thus must be replaced in the same piston groove. Ensure that the ring is the correct way up ie; stamped mark facing upwards and that the gaps are positoned over the locating pegs.
8   Examine each gudgeon pin for scores or stepped wear and renew if necessary. Check each gudgeon pin to piston fit; renew if necessary.

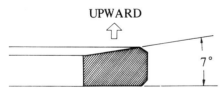

UPWARD

7°

Fig. 1.8. Keystone piston ring profile

26.7 The piston rings are marked to show the top surface

27 Small end bearings - examination

1   The small end bearings are of the caged needle roller type, and will seldom give trouble unless a lubrication failure has occurred. The gudgeon pins should be a good sliding fit in the bearings, without any play. The bearings must be tested whilst they are in place in each small eye. If play develops, a noticeable rattle will be heard when the engine is running, indicative of the need for bearing renewal.

28 Cylinder block and bores - examination and renovation

1   Clean out any mud and dirt from the fins to prevent overheating.
2   Check each bore for scores. If they are badly marked, they will have to be rebored and oversize pistons and rings fitted.
3   Bore wear can be measured using a cylinder bore dial test indicator (or a bore micrometer). If this is unavailable, it is possible to get an idea of the wear by measuring the end gap of a piston ring placed squarely in the bore, first at the bottom of the bore and secondly just below the limit of travel of the piston rings. If using a bore micrometer, the measurement should be taken between the front and rear of each barrel. When using the ring method, measure the ring gap with a set of feeler gauges. Subtract the smallest measurement from the largest (and divide by three is using the ring method of measurement). If the figures differ by more than 0.05 mm (0.002 in) a rebore is required.
Note: If the cylinders have been rebored and the port edges must be rounded off (top and bottom edges only) to prevent noise and ring wear. Use a file to obtain the measurements given in Fig. 1.9. Finish with 400 grade emery paper. Do not forget to wash the barrels afterwards, to remove all filings and emery dust.

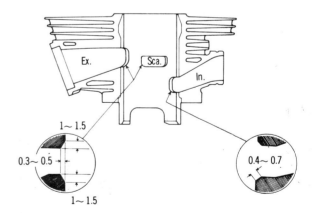

Ex.   Sca.   In.

1~1.5
0.3~0.5
0.4~0.7
1~1.5

Fig. 1.9. Port profiles

29 Piston/bore clearances - checking

1   Measure each piston diameter 16 mm (GT125) or 20 mm (GT185) above the piston skirt, perpendicular to the gudgeon pin hole.
2   Measure each bore, using an internal micrometer, and subtract from this figure the piston diameters obtained in the previous paragraph. Compare with the Specifications and renew if necessary.
3   Alternatively, if the appropriate measuring equipment is unavailable an approximate check of the clearances between the pistons and their bores can be made, using feeler gauges.

30 Clutch components - examination and renovation

1   Measure the full length of the clutch springs and compare
with the Specifications. Renew as a complete set, if necessary.
2   Measure the thickness of the clutch plates and compare with
the Specifications, renew as necessary. Also, check the clutch
plates for warpage by laying them on a flat surface. Measure the
warpage with a feeler gauge. Compare with the Specifications and
renew as necessary. Inspect the plain plates for scores and renew
as required.
3   Check the clutch plate tongues that locate in the clutch
housing are not worn; also examine the smaller teeth that locate
with the clutch centre. Any serious indentations or burrs mean
new parts will have to be obtained. Small burrs can be removed
with an oilstone or a fine cut file. Do not remove too much metal
however, since the tongues will then be of unequal width and
spacings and consequently will not take up the drive evenly. This
unevenness will cause the tongues to wear even more quickly and
probably also damage the clutch housing and centre.
4   Examine the clutch centre and housing grooves and dress
them if they are not too badly worn. If the grooves made by the
plates are left unattended, a sticky clutch action and possibly
clutch drag, will result.

30.4 Wear on the clutch housing should be dressed with a file

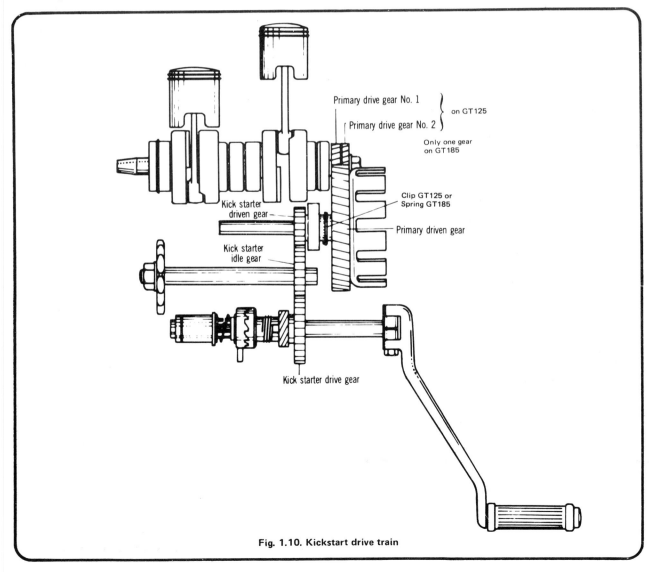

Fig. 1.10. Kickstart drive train

31 Gearbox and kickstart components - examination and renovation

1   Examine all the gear pinions, checking for chipped or broken teeth. Also check that the drive dogs are not worn or rounded. Renew as necessary. It is correct practice to always renew gears as a pair, so that they mesh correctly.

2   Check visually that the input and output shafts are not bent.

3   Check the gear selector forks/gear pinion groove clearance with a feeler gauge and compare with the Specifications. Renew as necessary.

4   Check that the gear selector forks are not bent or cracked, (particularly near the webbing).

5   Inspect the selector drum tracks for wear. In the unlikely event of excessive wear the drum will have to be renewed.

6   Measure the length of the gear selector shaft release spring. Compare with the Specifications and renew if necessary.

7   Check the condition of the kickstart ratchet teeth. If they are worn and rounded, the kickstart will slip.

32 Engine and gearbox reassembly - general

1   The importance of cleanliness cannot be overstressed. All components should be clean and lightly oiled. All bearings should be pre-lubricated.

2   Renew all gaskets and 'O' rings. If a gasket or 'O' ring is unobtainable, it is possible to use one of the modern silicon elastomer products such as Hermetite Instant Gasket.

3   Remove all traces of old gasket cement with a solvent such as methylated spirits. Ensure the jointing faces are smooth and not damaged. It is often convenient to use a little gasket cement to hold the gasket in position when reassembling. Use only a good quality, non-setting gasket cement, eg; Golden Hermetite, as required.

4   Ensure that the tools used are clean. The worst offenders for dirt and grit are sockets and this grit can easily find its way into the engine.

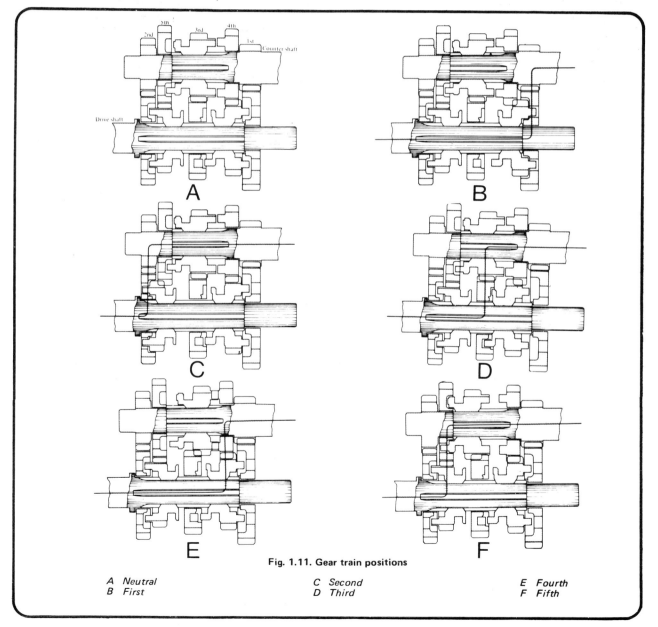

Fig. 1.11. Gear train positions

| A | Neutral | C | Second | E | Fourth |
| B | First | D | Third | F | Fifth |

33 Gear selectors - replacement

1   Enter the third gear selector shaft into the crankcase. Fit the selector fork followed by the neutral cam.
2   Replace the selector drum and forks, making sure that the selector with the largest strengthing web is placed on the left hand side of the engine. Replace the E-clips in the third gear selector shaft.
3   Replace the roller of the third gear selector fork and hook the neutral cam spring onto the oil baffle plate.
4   Replace both the guide pins and rollers in the other selector forks. Insert new split pins.
5   Replace the selector drum guide plate and tighten the two countersunk screws.

34 Kickstart shaft and components - assembly and replacement

1   Assemble the kickshaft components into the crankcase. Make sure to fit the belled washer in the direction shown in Fig. 1.12.
2   The kickstart mechanism is 'timed'. There is a punch mark on the ratchet dog and in one of the valleys of the shaft splines. When inserting the shaft into the crankcase, these two marks must align.
3   Check and renew if necessary, the rubber 'O'-ring and oil seal in the kickstart shaft bearing sleeve. Push the sleeve into the crankcase. Replace the retaining plate and tighten the two crosshead screws.
4   Inert the oil pump drive worm and gear/shaft into the crankcase.

33.1a Replace both the kickstart stop and oil baffle plate

33.1b Replace selector fork and neutral cam on shaft

Fig. 1.12. Fitting the kickstart belled washer

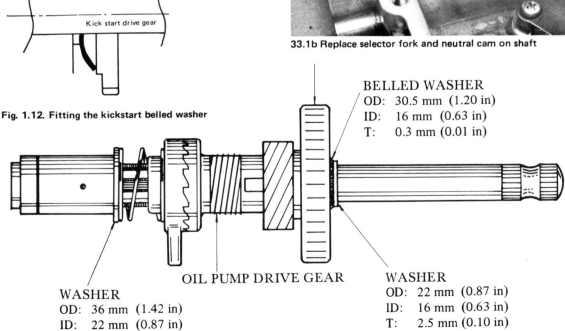

BELLED WASHER
OD: 30.5 mm (1.20 in)
ID: 16 mm (0.63 in)
T: 0.3 mm (0.01 in)

OIL PUMP DRIVE GEAR

WASHER
OD: 22 mm (0.87 in)
ID: 16 mm (0.63 in)
T: 2.5 mm (0.10 in)

WASHER
OD: 36 mm (1.42 in)
ID: 22 mm (0.87 in)
T: 1.5 mm (0.06 in)   **Fig. 1.13. Assembling the kickstart shaft**

33.2a Largest webbed selector fork goes on the left-hand side

33.2b Replace the left-hand and ...

33.2c ... right-hand E-clips

33.3 Replace roller in selector fork

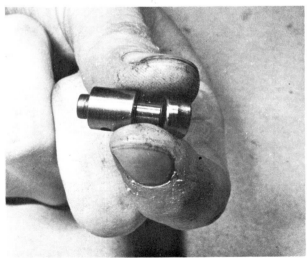

33.4a Assemble guide pin & roller before inserting them

33.4b Replace the split pins

34.1 The kickstart shaft & components

34.2a Align the two dot marks when replacing the shaft

34.2b Assemble the components and slide in the shaft

34.3a Check both the oil seals and ...

34.3b ... slide in the bearing sleeve

34.4 Replace the tachometer drive shaft

35 Gearbox - assembly

1 If the second gear on the input shaft has been removed, it must be pressed back onto the shaft; also, to prevent it from turning, a locking compound such as Torqueseal should be applied to the shaft, before pressing on the gear. The gear should be pressed onto the shaft to the dimensions given in Fig. 1.14. The gear must only be replaced on the shaft twice. After this, a new shaft must be obtained, to maintain the correct dimensional clearances.

2 When replacing the split needle roller bearing, make sure that the end with the largest cage is on the clutch side (see Fig. 1.15).

3 Do not forget any of the circlips or thrust washers, when reassembling the gear clusters; refer to Fig. 1.16.

35.1 Check length of input shaft when second gear has been pressed on

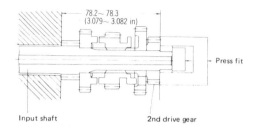

Fig. 1.14. Input shaft assembly dimensions

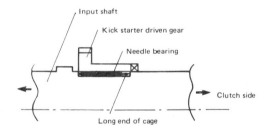

Fig. 1.15. Split needle roller cage position

35.2 Long end of cage must face clutch (outwards)

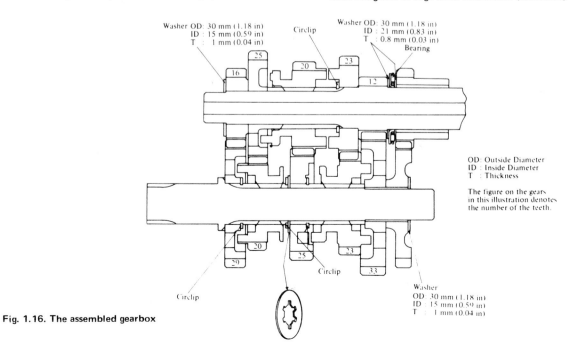

OD: Outside Diameter
ID : Inside Diameter
T : Thickness

The figure on the gears in this illustration denotes the number of the teeth.

Fig. 1.16. The assembled gearbox

36 Gearbox and crankshaft - replacement

1   Replace the previously assembled gearbox shafts into the top crankcase half.
2   Replace the bearing locating clips, washer and oil seals into the crankcase.
3   Replace the pre-assembled crankshaft into the crankcase. Make sure that the main bearing dowels locate in their recesses.

37 Joining the crankcases

1   Give both the mating surfaces of the crankcase a light smearing of gasket cement. Check again that all the components and oil seals are correctly located; pay particular attention to the bearing dowel pins.
2   Lower the bottom half onto the top. The two halves should line up and fit together; if not, check everything again and on no account use force.
3   Replace the seventeen bolts; tighten them in ascending numerical order.
4   Replace the bearing retainer plate on the gearbox input shaft. Fit and tighten the two crosshead screws.

38 Gear selector mechanism - replacement

1   Remove the gear selector pin retaining plate and replace the pawl plate. If the pins have been removed or have fallen out, they should be replaced as shown in Fig. 1.17.
2   Assemble the hairpin spring on the gear selector linkage, with the most bent spring end upwards. Slide the linkage into the crankcase and engage it in the selector drum.
3   Replace the pin retaining plate and tighten the countersunk crosshead screw.
4   Hook the positive stop lever spring onto the bearing retainer plate. Replace and tighten the shouldered pivot bolt.

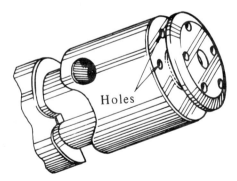

Fig. 1.17. Selector drum pin positions
The two longest pins must be fitted into the holes arrowed

39 Clutch and primary drive - assembly and replacement

GT125 model only
1   Replace the Woodruff key in the crankshaft.
2   Assemble the primary drive gear. Be careful to engage the spring tang in the hole. Replace the gear on the crankshaft, with the small quietening gear on the outside.
3   Lock the engine as described in Section 5 of this Chapter. Replace the lockwasher and tighten the nut. Knock over the tab of the lockwasher.

4   Fit the spring clip to the clutch housing and slide the housing onto the gearbox input shaft. When engaging the primary gears, tension the quietening gear against the spring tension to an amount equivalent to one tooth. Also, make sure that the clutch housing dogs engage with those of the kickstart idle gear. Finally, press home the housing making sure that the clip sits in the groove of the kickstart idle gear.
5   Screw the clutch springs into the clutch centre so that they are just flush with the surface. Replace the thrust washer followed by the clutch centre, lockwasher and nut. Place the engine in gear and hold the final drive sprocket so as to be able to tighten the clutch centre nut. Bend over the tabs of the lockwasher.
6   Replace the clutch plates in alternate fashion, starting with a friction plate.
7   Place the clutch pushrods, longest one first, followed by the clutch mushroom (where fitted).
8   Align the peripheral mark on the pressure plate with the mark on the edge of the clutch centre and replace the pressure plate.
9   Using either a pair of pliers or a bent piece of stout wire, pull out the clutch springs so as to enable their retaining pins to be replaced. It is advisable to cover the engine with a piece of rag during this procedure since it is very easy to drop one of the pins into the gearbox, which would then entail separating the crankcases again.

GT185 model only
10 Replace the Woodruff key in the crankshaft.
11 Replace the primary drive gear, lockwasher and nut on the crankshaft. Lock the engine as described in Section 5 of this Chapter and tighten the nut. Knock over the tab of the lockwasher.
12 Replace the spring on the gearbox input shaft or clip on the clutch housing if the model is GT185A and then the clutch housing: Make sure that the clutch housing dogs engage with those of the kickstart idle gear.
13 Screw the clutch springs into the clutch centre so that they are just flush with the surface. Replace the thrust washer followed by the clutch centre, lockwasher and nut. Place the engine in gear and hold the final drive sprocket so as to be able to tighten the clutch centre nut. Tighten the nut and bend over the tabs of the lockwasher.
14 Alternatively, replace the clutch plate starting with a friction plate.
15 Replace the clutch pushrod, rounded end in first.
16 Assemble the clutch operating rod into the pressure plate. Replace the pressure plate, making sure to align its peripheral mark with the one on the edge of the clutch centre.
17 Using either a pair of pliers or a bent piece of stout wire, pull out the clutch springs so as to enable the pins to be replaced. It is advisable to cover the engine with a piece of rag during this procedure since it is very easy to drop one of the pins into the gearbox which would then entrail separating the crankcases again.

40 Kickstart return spring - replacement

1   Replace the shaped spacer (GT185 model only) and turn the kickstart shaft fully clockwise. Twist the spring anti-clockwise about ½ a turn and insert the spring tang into the hole provided in the kickstart shaft.
2   Slide in the plastic sleeve and replace the large washer.

41 Primary drive cover - replacement

1   Use a new gasket and refit the primary drive cover. Before replacing it, check the condition of the oil seals and renew, if necessary.
2   Fit and tighten the ten screws in an even and diagonal sequence.

36.2a Replace the washer ...

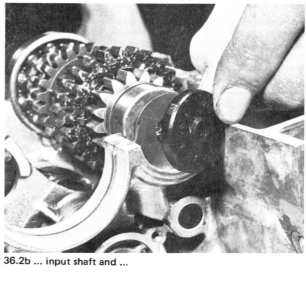

36.2b ... input shaft and ...

36.2c ... output shaft oil seal ...

36.2d ... also the bearing retaining clips of the bearbox and ...

36.2e ... crankshaft

36.3 Make sure the dowel pins locate in the recesses

37.1 Check the oil way is clear

37.2 Replace the bottom crankcase half on inverted assembly

37.4 Replace the bearing retaining plate

38.1 Fit the selector panel plate

38.2a The correct way to assemble the gearlever hairpin spring

38.2b Slide in the gear lever shaft

38.4 Hook positive stop lever on to bearing retainer and

39.2a Engage spring tang in the hole of smaller gear and ...

39.2b ... replace the circlip

39.5a Screw in the clutch springs until ...

39.5b ... they are flush with the back of clutch

39.5c Replace the clutch centre and ...

39.5d ... the lockwasher and centre nut ...

39.6 Replace the clutch plates in alternate fashion

39.7 Insert the clutch mushroom (GT125)

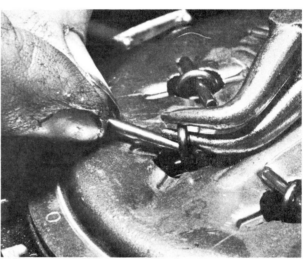

39.9 Raise the springs and insert the pins

40.2a Replace the kickstart spring, sleeve and ...

40.2b ... thrust washer

41.1 Check condition of seal before replacing cover

42.1b ... cam and rotor bolt

42 Alternator or dynamo/starter and cover - replacement

1   Refit the Woodruff key to the crankshaft and fit the
alternator and cam (GT125 model), or armature and cam
(GT185 model). Torque tighten the centre nut to 90 - 140 kg
cm (6.6 - 10. lb ft) whilst holding the engine as described in
Section 5 of this Chapter.
2   Replace the stator (GT125) or field coil (GT185) assembly
making sure to locate its slot with the pin the crankcase.
3   Replace and tighten the three screws.
4   Before replacing the cover, the contact breaker gap should
be checked and the ignition timing see Section 5 of Chapter 3.
Use a new gasket when replacing the cover and tighten the screws
evenly.

43 Neutral light switch - replacement

1   If the wiper contact has not already been replaced, it should
be fitted to the selector drum. Make sure to locate the tang before
tightening the screw.
2   Use a new gasket and replace the switch body. Do not
overtighten the three screws.
3   Reconnect the wire to the switch body.

43.1 Replace the neutral light switch wiper

42.1a Replace the rotor and ...

43.2 Do not overtighten the three screws

44 Final drive sprocket - replacement

1   Replace the final drive sprocket over the splined gearbox output shaft. Fit the locking plate and align the bolt holes with those in the sprocket.
2   Fit a new lockwasher and tighten the two bolts. Do not forget to bend over the tabs of the lockwashers.

45 Gearlever linkage - replacement

1   Lubricate the seal in the kickstart sleeve with a little graphite or molybdenum grease. Align the dot marks, on the lever and spline, made when dismantling, and fit the lever. Replace the bolt and tighten.

46 Oil pump and cover - replacement

1   Replace the oil distribution manifold onto the crankcase.
2   Use two washers on each of the oil pipe banjos and refit the banjo bolts. Do not overtighten them. Pump two-stroke oil into the manifold and pipes, using a pressure oil can to displace the air and prime the pipes with oil.
3   Fit new 'O'-rings to the manifold. Replace the drive pin in the oil pump shaft and refit the oil pump. Replace and evenly tighten the three screws.
4   Replace the cover over the pump. Fit and tighten the two screws and one bolt. Do **not** fit the inspection cover plate yet.

47 Tachometer drive replacement

1   Check the condition of the rubber 'O'-ring in the tachometer drive shaft and renew if necessary. Slide the shaft into its sleeve, making sure to align the indent with the bolt hole. Fit and tighten the securing bolt.

48 Cylinder block and pistons - replacement

1   Clean all the gasket faces. Make sure that the oilways in the crankcase at the rear of each cylinder barrel is clear and not clogged with gasket compound, likewise the mating holes in each cylinder barrel itself.
2   Fit new cylinder base gaskets and lubricate the big end bearings with a little two-stroke oil.
3   Slide in the pre-lubricated small end bearings.
4   Fit the pistons and rings with the arrow on the piston tops pointing forwards, towards the exhaust port. Fit the piston circlips. Always use new circlips and check that they have seated properly in their grooves. **Do not use the old circlips** since they will have lost some of their spring tension and may jump out and cause the engine to seize.
5   Lubricate the piston rings and align their gaps on the locating pegs. Slide each cylinder barrel over the studs and piston, whilst compressing the piston rings with the fingers to facilitate entry.
6   On the GT185 model, replace the cylinder base nuts and washers. Tighten each of these nuts in a diagonal sequence.

49 Cylinder head and cover - replacement

1   Fit new cylinder head gaskets or, if undamaged, anneal the old ones by heating them to red heat and quenching them by dropping them edge on into water. **Do not use any gasket cement.**
2   Replace the cylinder head and torque tighten the nuts in a even and diagonal sequence (200 - 250 k/cm or 14 - 18 lb/ft).
3   Check the condition of the rubber grommets and renew

them if they have perished. Replace the cover and tighten the four screws.
4   Squirt a little two-stroke oil down the plug holes and turn the engine over a few times. Replace the spark plugs.

50 Refitting the engine/gearbox into the frame

1   The engine/gearbox should be refitted into the frame by reversing the procedure given in Section 3 of this Chapter. Do not forget to fit a new exhaust pipe gaskets.
2   When refitting the kickstart and gear lever, use a little thread locking compound eg; Torqueseal, on the pinch bolts; this will prevent the levers from working loose and thereby damaging the splines.

51 Clutch adjustment

1   Although the GT125 and GT185 models have different clutch operating mechanisms, the adjustment technique is similar. The only difference is where the adjustment is made; on the GT125 model the adjustment is behind the rear left-hand cover, while that on the GT185 model is located behind the inspection cover of the primary drive engine cover (right-hand side).
2   Adjust the clutch cable free play to approximately 4 mm (1/3 in.).
3   Slacken the lock nut and turn the screw clockwise until resistance is felt. Back off the screw by between ¼ - ½ turn. Retighten the lock nut, whilst holding the screw. After adjusting check that the clutch is operating correctly ie; not slipping or binding.

52 Final adjustments

1   Check the contact breaker gap and ignition timing. See Chapter 3 Sections 5 and 6 respectively.
2   Adjust the oil pump cable and bleed the system. See Chapter 2, Section 11. Replace and tighten the inspection cover plate.
3   Replace the spark plug caps.
4   Refill the transmission with oil; see Chapter 2, Section 15 for further details. Check there is sufficient engine oil in the side-mounted tank.

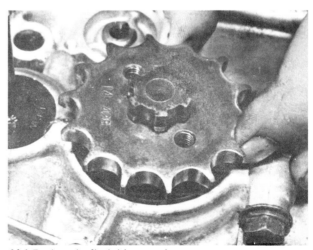

44.1 Replace the final drive sprocket

44.2 Do not forget to bend over the tabs of the lockwashers

46.2 Replace the banjo bolts, using two new washers on each

46.3 Replace the oil pump drive pin before fitting pump

47.1 The screw must align with indent in the driveshaft

48.1a Make sure that both the hole in the crankcase and ...

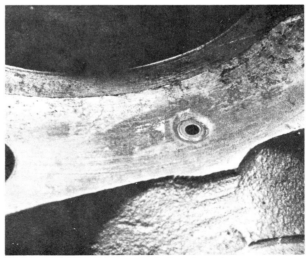
48.1b ... the drilling in the cylinder barrel are clear

48.3 Insert the small end bearing

48.4a The piston must be replaced with the arrow pointing forwards.

48.4b Use new circlips, NEVER the original

48.5a Align the ring gaps over the locating pegs and ...

48.5b ... slide on the cylinder barrel

49.2 Torque tighten the nuts in the sequence shown

50.1a Fit a new exhaust pipe gasket

50.1b Do not forget the engine earthing wire (GT185 model only)

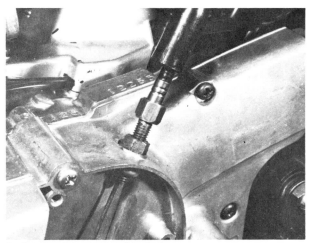

51.2 Adjust for correct cable slack

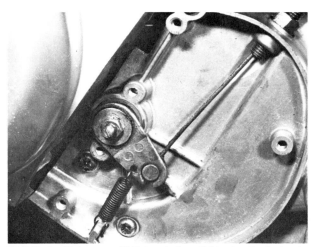

51.3 Back off the screw ¼-½ turn before tightening the locknut

53 Starting and running the rebuilt engine

1 When the initial start-up is made, run the engine slowly for the first few minutes, especially if the engine has been rebored or a new crankshaft fitted. Check that all the controls function correctly and that there are no oil leaks before taking the machine on the road. The exhaust will emit a high proportion of white smoke during the first few miles, as the excess oil used whilst the engine was reassembled is burnt away. The volume of smoke should gradually diminish until only the customary light blue haze is observed during normal running. It is wise to carry a spare spark plug during the first run, since the existing plug may oil up due to the temporary excess of oil.

2 Remember that a good seal between the pistons and the cylinder barrels is essential for the correct functioning of the engine. A rebored two-stroke engine will require more careful running-in, over a long period, than its four-stroke counterpart. There is a far greater risk of engine seizure during the first hundred miles if the engine is permitted to work hard.

3 Do not tamper with the exhaust system or run the engine without the baffle fitted to the silencer. Unwarranted changes in the exhaust system will have a very marked effect on engine performance, invariably for the worst. The same advice to dispensing with the air cleaner or the air cleaner element.

4 Do not on any account add oil to the petrol under the mistaken belief that a little extra oil will improve the engine lubrication. Apart from creating excess smoke, the addition of oil will make the mixture much weaker, with the consequent risk of overheating and engine seizure. The oil pump alone should provide full engine lubrication.

Fault diagnosis Engine, Clutch and Gearbox on following pages 42 and 43

54 Fault diagnosis - engine

Symptom	Cause	Remedy
Engine will not start	Defective spark plug	Remove plugs and lay on cylinder head Check whether spark occurs when engine is kicked over
	Dirty or closed contact breaker points	Check condition of points and whether gap is correct
	Air leak at crankcase or worn oil seals around crankshaft	Check whether mixture is reaching the spark plugs
	Clutch slip	Check and adjust clutch
Engine runs unevenly	Ignition and/or fuel system fault	Check systems as though engine will not start
	Blowing cylinder head gasket	Leak should be evident from oil leakage where gas escapes.
	Incorrect ignition timing	Check timing and reset if necessary
Lack of power	Incorrect ignition timing	See above
	Fault in fuel system	Check system and filler cap vent
	Blowing head gasket	See above
	Choked silencer	Clean out baffles
High fuel/oil consumption	Cylinder barrels in need of rebore and o/s pistons	Fit new rings and pistons after rebore
	Oil leaks or air leaks from damaged gaskets or oil seals	Trace source of leak and replace damage gaskets or seals
Excessive mechanical noise	Worn cylinder barrels (piston slap)	Rebore and fit o/s pistons
	Worn small end bearings (rattle)	Renew bearings and gudgeon pins
	Worn big-end bearings (knock)	Fit a replacement crankshaft assembly
	Worn main bearings (rumble)	Fit new journal bearings and seals
Engine overheats and fades	Pre-ignition and/or weak mixture	Check carburettor settings. Check also whether plug grades correct
	Lubrication failure	Check oil pump setting and whether oil tank is empty

55 Fault diagnosis - clutch

Symptom	Cause	Remedy
Engine speed increases but machine does not respond	Clutch slip	Check clutch adjustment for pressure on pushrod. Also free play at handlebar lever Check condition of clutch plate linings, also free length of clutch springs, replace if necessary
Difficulty in engaging gears. Gear changes jerky and machine creeps forward, even when clutch is fully withdrawn	Clutch drag	Check clutch adjustment for too much free play
	Clutch plates worn and/or clutch drum	Check for burrs on clutch plate tongues or indentations in clutch drum slots. Dress with file
	Clutch assembly loose on mainshaft	Check tightness of retaining nut. If loose, fit new tab washer and retighten
Operating action stiff	Damaged, trapped or frayed control cable	Check cable and renew if necessary. Make sure cable is lubricated and has no sharp bends
	Bent pushrod	Renew

56 Fault diagnosis - gearbox

Symptom	Cause	Remedy
Difficulty in engaging gears	Gear selector forks bent Gear cluster assembled incorrect	Renew Check that thrust washers are located correctly
Machine jumps out of gear	Worn dogs on ends of gear pinions Selector drum pawls stuck	Renew pinions involved Free pawl assembly
Gear lever does not return to normal position	Broken return spring	Renew spring
Kickstart does not return when engine is turned over or started	Broken or poorly tensioned return spring	Renew spring or retension
Kickstart slips	Kickstart drive pinion internals worn badly	Renew all worn parts

Chapter 2 Fuel system and lubrication

Contents

Specifications

Carburettor

	GT125	GT185
Make	Mikuni	Mikuni
Type	VM18SC (L models) VM19SC (M and A models)	VM20SC
Main jet	70 (L and M models) 72.5 (A models)	72.5
Needle	4F19-3	4D17-3
Needle position (grooves from the top)	3	3
Needle jet	N-8 (L models) 0-0 (M models) 0-3 (A models)	N-5 (K & L models) N-4 (M & R models)
Throttle slide cutaway	2.5	1.5
Pilot jet	25	20
Pilot outlet	1.0	1.2
Pilot air adjusting screw (turns out)	1½	1
Float needle valve	1.3	1.2
Starter jet	50	40
Float level	19.9 ± 1 mm	19.9 ± 1 mm

Oil pump performance

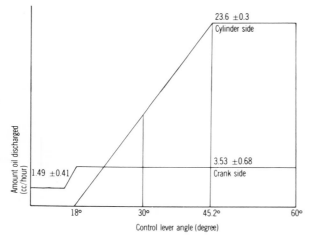

Fig. 2.1. Oil pump performance curve, GT125 model

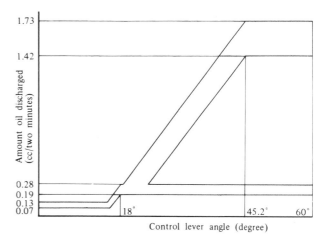

Fig. 2.2. Oil pump performance curve, GT185 model

Transmission oil capacity (all models) ... ... 800 cc (1.41 Imp pt)

1 The fuel system - general description

1   The fuel from the petrol tank is fed via a tap, incorporating two separate filters and a sediment bowl, to the two Mikuni carburettors. The carburettors are of the fixed choke type, with a cylindrical throttle slide. A lever operated cold start device is fitted. An air cleaner of the oil impregnated foam filter type is fitted.

2 Petrol tank - removal and replacement

1   Turn off the petrol tap and disconnect the fuel pipe.
2   Hinge up the dual seat and unhook the rubber clip from the rear of the tank. The tank can now be removed by lifting it up and backwards.
3   Check the tank for splits and leaks. Also check the condition of the rubbers and renew them if they show any signs of deterioration. On no account omit the rubbers or rigidly mount the tank because of the risk of it splitting from vibration.
4   Replace by reversing the above procedure.

3 Fuel tap - removal and renovation

1   If required, the complete tap can be removed, after draining the tank, by undoing the two bolts. This then provides access to the two gauze filters which should be cleaned by washing them in petrol.
2   The sediment bowl of the fuel tap should periodically be cleaned out. It is removed by unscrewing, which gives access to the fuel filter without need to either drain the tank or detach the tap. Clean the filter with petrol. Check the condition of the 'O'-ring seal before replacing the bowl.
3   If the fuel tap is leaking, it is most likely due to deterioration of, or damage to, the rubber seal. Access to this is obtained by removing the two lever retaining plate screws, followed by the plate and tap lever. Renew the seal. In this case it will be necessary to drain the tank of petrol first.

4 Air cleaner - cleaning

1   The air cleaner is of the oil impregnated foam type. Access to the two elements is made by removing the side covers and undoing the screw on the left-hand end of the filter box. Remove the two end covers and withdraw the filter elements.
2   Carefully remove the foam from its supporting cylinder, wash it in petrol and soak the element in two-stroke oil. Then squeeze out the excess.
3   Check that the foam is not damaged or holed. Replace the filters in the filter box and reassemble them by reversing the above procedure.
4   Never use a machine with a damaged element or without an air filter, since this weakens the mixture, causing over-heating and possible seizure.

5 Carburettor - removal

1   Turn off the petrol and disconnect the petrol pipe.
2   Unscrew both the carburettor tops and carefully pull out the throttle slides and needles. Label both the slides and needles so that they can be replaced in the same carburettors.
3   Slacken the two air filter hose clips and pull off the hoses.
4   Depending on the model, either slacken the hose clips on the engine side and pull each carburettor out of its hose or slacken the bolt in each carburettor clip and slide each carburettor off the inlet manifold.
5   Replacement is a reversal of the above. Be careful not to cross thread the carburettor tops when replacing them.

2.2 Petrol tank is held by rubber clip at rear and ...

2.3 ... two rubber cushions at front

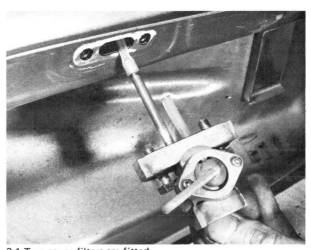

3.1 Two gauze filters are fitted

3.2 The sediment bowl is removed by unscrewing

4.1 A oil wetted foam filter is utilised

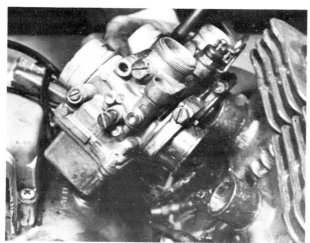

5.4 Slide carburettors off inlet stubs

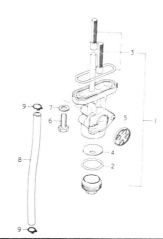

Fig. 2.3. Fuel tap

1 Complete tap assembly
2 Rubber gasket
3 Tubular filter - 2 off
4 Flat filter
5 Lever rubber gasket
6 Bolt - 2 off
7 Fibre washer - 2 off
8 Petrol pipe
9 Wire hose clip -
   2 off

6 Carburettors - dismantling, examination and reassembly

1   Dismantle each carburettor separately, as described, so that parts cannot be interchanged. Invert the carburettor and remove the four screws that retain the float bowl. Lift off the float bowl. Note that the cold start jet is located in the float bowl and is non-replaceable.
2   Slide out the float pivot pin and lift out the float. Unscrew the needle valve assembly; note that there is a fibre washer fitted underneath.
3   Use a screwdriver to remove the main jet and a small ring spanner for the emulsion tube/needle jet. The venturi tube is a press fit in the carburettor body and does not normally require removal.
4   Unscrew the pilot jet.
5   If required, remove both the throttle stop and the pilot jet air adjusting screws. Check that the screws are not bent and that the air adjuster screw is not scored. Also check the condition of the 'O'-rings. Renew, if necessary.
6   The cold start device is fitted only to the left-hand carburettor the mixture being fed to the right-hand carburettor via a inter-connecting pipe. Remove the device by unscrewing the top nut. Check the condition of the seal on the bottom of the plunger. If it shows signs of deterioration, renew the plunger. Also check the condition of the 'O' ring and renew as necessary.
7   The throttle slide is removed from the cable by pushing the cable in and moving it outwards. The needle is retained by a clip and positioned by an E-clip in one of its five grooves.
8   Check the condition of the fibre carburettor/inlet stub sleeve. If it is cracked or damaged, it must be renewed. On models fitted with a rubber connecting hose instead of a fibre sleeve, check that the hose is not perished or cracked.
9   Check that the needle is not bent by rolling it on a flat surface. If it has worn, obtain a new replacement and also renew the needle jet.
10 Check that the throttle slide is not badly worn or scored. Renew if necessary. If the throttle slide is badly scored check the condition of the carburettor body, which may also require renewal.
11 Do not use wire or any other thin metal object to clear a blocked jet. The hole can easily become enlarged or mis-shapen, which will seriously affect the flow of fuel. To clean the jets blow them out with compressed air eg; a foot pump.
12 Check the float assembly for leaks by shaking it. If petrol can be heard inside a float, a replacement will have to be obtained.
13 To reassemble, reverse the above procedure. Do not over-tighten the jets and renew the gaskets, if damaged. Particular attention should be paid to the carburettor/cylinder barrel 'O' ring, at the joint with the inlet port. Refit the needle jet with the cutaway facing forwards (towards the engine). Before replacing the float bowl, check the float height, see the next section.

6.2a The jets are exposed, after removing float bowl

6.2b The needle can be lifted out of seating

6.3a Unscrew the main jet followed by ...

6.3b ... the emulsion tube/needle jet

6.5a Unscrew the throttle stop screw and ...

6.5b ... the pilot air adjuster screw

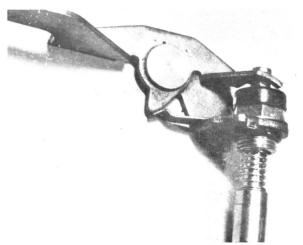

6.6 The cold start device is removed as a unit

6.7a Remove the throttle cable from slide

6.7b A wire clip retains the needle which is ...

6.7c ... positioned by a circlip

6.13 The cutaway must face forwards

7 Carburettor - float height adjustment

1   Remove the float bowl and with the carburettor upside down lower the float needle until its tang just touches the needle valve. Measure the distance between the bottom of the float and the carburettor gasket face (the gasket must be removed). Compare with the Specifications and adjust, if necessary, by carefully bending the tang.

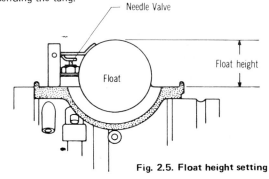

Fig. 2.5. Float height setting

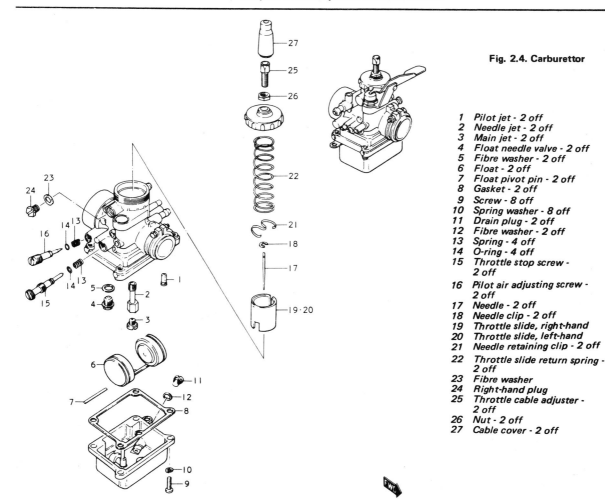

Fig. 2.4. Carburettor

1 Pilot jet - *2 off*
2 Needle jet - *2 off*
3 Main jet - *2 off*
4 Float needle valve - *2 off*
5 Fibre washer - *2 off*
6 Float - *2 off*
7 Float pivot pin - *2 off*
8 Gasket - *2 off*
9 Screw - *8 off*
10 Spring washer - *8 off*
11 Drain plug - *2 off*
12 Fibre washer - *2 off*
13 Spring - *4 off*
14 O-ring - *4 off*
15 Throttle stop screw - *2 off*
16 Pilot air adjusting screw - *2 off*
17 Needle - *2 off*
18 Needle clip - *2 off*
19 Throttle slide, right-hand
20 Throttle slide, left-hand
21 Needle retaining clip - *2 off*
22 Throttle slide return spring - *2 off*
23 Fibre washer
24 Right-hand plug
25 Throttle cable adjuster - *2 off*
26 Nut - *2 off*
27 Cable cover - *2 off*

8 Carburettor settings - general

1 Some of the carburettor settings, such as the sizes of the needle jets, main jets and needle position etc, are pre-determined by the manufacturer. Under normal circumstances it is unlikely that these settings will require modification, even though there is provision made. If a change appears necessary, it can often be attributed to a developing engine fault.

2 As an approximate guide, the pilot jet setting controls engine speed up to 1/8 throttle. The throttle slide cut-a-way controls engine speed from 1/8 to ¼ throttle and the position of the needle in the slide from ¼ to ¾ throttle. The size of the main jet is responsible for engine speed at the final ¾ to full throttle. It should be added however that these are only guide lines. There is no clearly defined demarkation line due to a certain amount of overlap that occurs between the carburettor components involved.

3 Always keep slightly on the side of a rich mixture, since a weak mixture will cause the engine to overheat. Reference to Chapter 3 will show how the condition of the spark plugs can be interpreted with some experience as a reliable guide to carburettor mixture length.

9 Carburettor adjustments - synchronisation and tickover speed

1 Before adjusting the carburettors, the throttle slides must be synchronised ie; the throttle slides must both start to lift at the same time. Adjust both the throttle cables so that they have an identical amount of free-play which should be within 0.5 - 1.0 mm (0.02 - 0.04 in). Adjustment of the cables is made by the adjusters on top of the carburettors. The cable between the twist grip and the junction box should also be adjusted to give the same amount of free-play.

NB. It is imperative to check the oil pump cable adjustment setting after adjusting the carburettors since this setting will probably have altered (see Section 11 of this Chapter).

2 It is best to regard each carburettor and cylinder separately when adjusting the carburettors. First, make sure that there are no air leaks and that the air filter is clean. The engine should be at its normal working temperature before making any adjustments.

3 Remove the spark plug from the cylinder that is not having its carburettor adjusted. Screw in the pilot air adjusting screw until it just seats, then unscrew 1½ turns. Make sure that there is some slack in the throttle cables.

4 Start the engine and adjust the throttle stop screw for a fast tickover. Turn the pilot air adjuster (clockwise gives a richer mixture and vice versa) to obtain the fastest tickover. Note the rpm reading on the tachometer.

5 Repeat the procedure with the other carburettor, after replacing the corresponding spark plug and removing the other one. Adjust the throttle stop screw so as to obtain the same rpm. reading as before.

6 With both plugs in position, start the engine again. It will now be found that the tickover speed will be too fast. Unscrew the throttle stop screws of each carburettor by an **identical amount**, to obtain a satisfactory tickover speed.

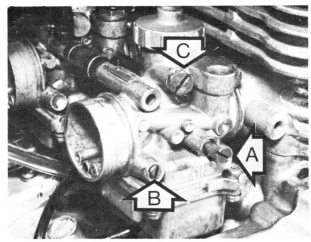

9.4a The throttle stop screw
9.4b the pilot aire adjusting screw
9.4c Oil pump aligning plug

11.3 Mark must be at the top of the hole, not as shown

11.4 Pump marks should align when slide is in correct position

10 Lubrication system - general description

1   The GT125 and GT185 models have two separate lubrication systems; one for the crankshaft and pistons (C.C.I system) and the other for the transmission.
2   The C.C.I. lubrication system comprises an oil tank which gravity feeds a variable rate pump with oil of the correct viscosity (SAE30). The pump is driven via a worm gear from the kickstart shaft. The oil is fed to a manifold, from where it is distributed to the left-hand and middle main bearings, and also into the inlet manifold, via a drilling in each cylinder barrel. The right-hand main bearing is lubricated from the transmission oil. The pump discharge rate is controlled by the throttle opening and therefore the amount of oil is regulated to that required by the engine. This system is far more economical and free from the inherent problems of the old petrol/oil mixture that at one time was commonplace in two strokes.
3   The transmission is lubricated by the wet sump method and the oil requires only routine checking and changing at the recommended intervals. On no account must two-stroke oil be used in **this** lubrication system.

11 Oil pump - operating principle and adjustment

1   The oil pump is mechanically driven by a shaft from the bottom of the gearbox. This shaft also operates the tachometer drive.
2   The pump works on the rotating principle with a control arm inside the body have a valve and connected with spring loaded plungers, to distribute the oil through the feed hoses. The cam is connected to a pump control lever that in turn is connected by means of a control cable to the twist grip throttle. More oil is fed to the engine as the engine speed increases, by the opening of the throttle.
3   The oil pump should be set after the carburettors have been adjusted. Remove the aligning plug hole in the right-hand carburettor. Rotate the twist grip until the aligning mark on the throttle slide is positioned at the top of the hole (see Fig. 2.7).
4   Check that the mark on the oil pump operating arm is aligned with the mark on the oil pump body. Adjust as necessary, using the cable adjuster in the oil pump cover. Do not forget to retighten the locknut, after adjustment.

12 Oil pump - bleeding the system

1   If air is present in the main oil line to the oil pump (this could happen if oil tank is allowed to empty or reach a very low level) refill the oil tank to the correct level with engine oil. This level should be checked through the sight glass in the oil tank.
2   Remove the cover over the oil pump by undoing the two roundhead screws. The oil pump is now exposed. Loosen the oil pump bleeder screw about 1 turn to 1½ turns and allow oil to seep out until all air bubbles have been expelled from the oil in the pipe.
3   To expell air in the discharge side of the pump, proceed as follows: Remove the oil pump and using a pressure oil filler fitted with a spout, squirt clean engine oil in the oil pipes supplying the engine. Pump until all the air is expelled and the pipes are full of oil. Then reinstall the oil pump and reconnect the oil feed banjo and pipe, after checking the main feed pipes is still primed with oil.
4   If there is only a little air in the system, this can be expelled by holding the oil control level fully the open whilst keeping the engine running at about 2,000 rpm until all the air bubbles disappear.

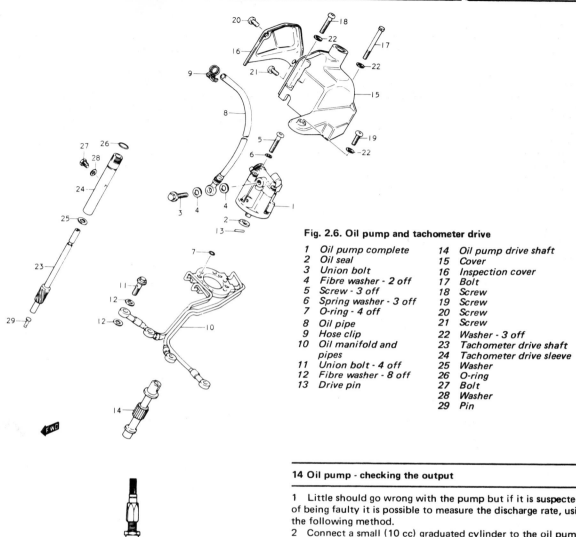

Fig. 2.6. Oil pump and tachometer drive

1	Oil pump complete	14	Oil pump drive shaft
2	Oil seal	15	Cover
3	Union bolt	16	Inspection cover
4	Fibre washer - 2 off	17	Bolt
5	Screw - 3 off	18	Screw
6	Spring washer - 3 off	19	Screw
7	O-ring - 4 off	20	Screw
8	Oil pipe	21	Screw
9	Hose clip	22	Washer - 3 off
10	Oil manifold and pipes	23	Tachometer drive shaft
11	Union bolt - 4 off	24	Tachometer drive sleeve
12	Fibre washer - 8 off	25	Washer
13	Drive pin	26	O-ring
		27	Bolt
		28	Washer
		29	Pin

14 Oil pump - checking the output

1   Little should go wrong with the pump but if it is suspected of being faulty it is possible to measure the discharge rate, using the following method.
2   Connect a small (10 cc) graduated cylinder to the oil pump inlet pipe. Fill the cylinder with two-stroke oil.
3   Start the engine and keep it running at a constant speed of 2000 rpm ± 100 rpm. Raise the oil pump lever until it is fully open and measure the amount of oil used. The engine should use, after two minutes, between 0.82 - 1.12 cc (GT125) and 1.61 - 2.01 cc (GT185). Whilst making the measurement, it is imperative to keep the engine speed constant, since the discharge rate is controlled by the engine speed.

15 Transmission oil - changing

1   The transmission oil can be drained by removing both the filler cap and the drain plug, preferably when the oil is warm. A drain tray of at least 800 cc (1.4 Imp. pts) capacity will be required to hold the old oil.
2   Replace the drain plug and washer. Fill the gearbox with 800 cc of oil (ie; until the correct level is shown on the dipstick). The oil level should be maintained between the F & L lines. Do not push the filler cap in when checking the level; it should rest on top of the hole. The machine should be placed on level ground when checking the oil level.
3   On some models, an oil level screw is fitted in the primary drive cover, near the kickstart shaft. To save measuring out the oil, remove the screw and fill with oil until it just issues out of the hole. Do not forget to replace the screw, after all excess oil has drained off.

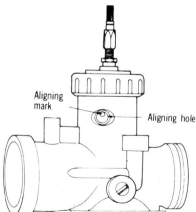

Aligning mark

Aligning hole

Fig. 2.7. Carburettor/oil pump aligning mark - correct position

13 Oil pump - dismantling

1   It is unlikely that the pump will require any attention due to the very low wear rate. Also, due to the precision fit of the components, it is not recommended that the pump be dismantled unnecessarily. Check the condition of the oil seal and renew it, if necessary.
2   Oil pump removal is described in Chapter 1, Section 9.

16 Exhaust system - cleaning

1　The exhaust system is often the most neglected part of any two-stroke despite the fact that it has quite a pronounced effect on performance. It is essential that the exhaust system is inspected and cleaned out at regular intervals because the exhaust gases from a two-stroke engine has a particularly oily nature which will encourage the build-up of sludge. This will cause back pressures and affect the 'breathing' of the engine.

2　Cleaning is made easy by fitting the silencers with detachable baffles, held in position by a screw which passes through each silencer end. If the screw is withdrawn, the baffles can be drawn out of position for cleaning.

3　A wash with a petrol/paraffin mix will remove most of the oil and carbon deposits, but if the build-up is severe it is permissible to heat the baffles with a blow lamp and burn off the carbon and old oil.

4　At less frequent intervals, such as when the engine requires decarbonising, it is advisable also to clean out the exhaust pipes. This will prevent the gradual build-up of an internal coating of carbon and oil, over an extended period.

5　Do not run the machine with the baffles detached or with a quite different type of silencer fitted. The standard production silencers have been designed to give the best possible performance whilst subduing the exhaust note. Although a modified exhaust system may give the illusion of greater speed as a result of the changed exhaust note, the chances are that performance will have suffered accordingly.

6　When replacing the exhaust system, use new sealing rings at the exhaust port joints and check that the baffle retaining screws in the silencer ends are tightened fully.

16.2a Remove the baffle screw ...

16.2b ... withdraw the baffle assembly

17 Fault diagnosis - fuel system and lubrication

Symptom	Cause	Remedy
Engine gradually fades and stops	Fuel starvation	Check vent hole in filler cap and clear if blocked Sediment in filter bowl or blocking float needle. Dismantle and clean
Engine runs badly, black smoke from exhausts	Carburettor flooding	Dismantle and clean carburettor. Look for punctured float
Engine lacks response and overheats	Weak mixture Air filter disconnected or hoses split	Check for partial blockage in fuel/carburettor Reconnect or repair
White smoke from exhaust	Oil pump setting incorrect, too much oil passing Incorrect oil in oil tank	Check and reset oil pump Drain and refill with recommended grade
General lack of response to varying throttle openings	Blocked exhaust system	Remove silencer baffles and clean

Chapter 3 Ignition system

Contents

Specifications

Spark plug			GT125	GT185
Type			NGK B8HS	NGK B8HS
Gap			0.6 - 0.7 mm	0.6 - 0.7 mm
			(0.024 - 0.028 in)	(0.024 - 0.028 in)
Ignition timing:				
Standard mm BTDC			1.95	1.83 (K and L models)
$^{\circ}$ BTDC			22	2.63 (M & A models)
Contact breaker points gap			0.3 - 0.4 mm	0.3 - 0.4 mm
			(0.012 - 0.016 in)	(0.012 - 0.016 in)
Condenser capacity			0.16 - 0.20 uF	0.22 uF

1 General description

1 A conventional contact breaker coil igniton system is used.
The contact breaker is operated by a cam on the alternator rotor.
The opening and closing of a contact breaker every revolution
causes a magnetic field in the primary winding of the ignition
coil to build up and then collapse. This induces a high voltage in
the secondary winding which causes the spark to occur across the
electrodes of the spark plug concerned.

2 Ignition coil - function

1 The ignition coil consists of primary and secondary windings
mounted on a soft iron core. It operates in conjunction with the
contact breaker to convert low voltage from the primary coil
into the high voltage necessary for the spark.
2 The Suzuki GT125 and GT185 models have a twin coil unit,
each cylinder having its own ignition system. The assembly is
enclosed within the top frame tubes.

3 Ignition coil - locating and checking

1 The ignition coil assembly is located under the petrol tank, which
has to be removed to give access (see Chapter 2, Section 2).
2 The ignition coil is a sealed unit, designed to give long
service without need for attention. If a weak spark, no spark at
all or difficult starting causes the performance of the coil

assembly to be suspect, it should be tested by a Suzuki agent or
an auto-electrical specialist who will have the appropriate test
equipment. A faulty coil must be renewed since it is not possible
to effect a satisfactory repair.
3 A defective condenser can give the illusion of a faulty coil
and for this reason it is advisable to investigate the condition of
the condenser before condemning the ignition coil.

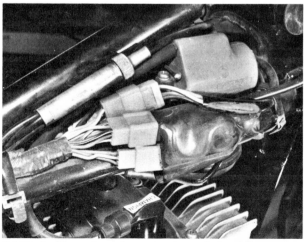

3.1 The ingition coils are located underneath the tank

4 Condenser - function and location

1 The condenser has two functions. Firstly it reduces sparking at the contact breaker points (and hence prevents rapid wear of the points). Its second and more important function is to greatly increase the induced voltage in the secondary windings of the coil and hence the strength of the high tension spark at break. In practice, without the condenser the spark is very weak and the bike does not run smoothly. As each cylinder of the Suzuki GT125 and GT185 models has its own ignition circuits, two condensers are fitted.
2 The condensers are located on the stator plate and are each held in position by one crosshead screw.
3 If a condenser is suspected of malfunctioning, it should be removed and replaced with a new spare. There is no easy means of checking a condenser without the appropriate test equipment and it is more convenient to cross check by substitution, especially in view of the low cost of this component.
4 The usual signs of a defective condenser are a weak 'thin' spark and the blackened, burnt appearance of the faces of the contact breaker points, due to arcing. A small amount of arcing is inevitable, but never an intense spark at every opening and closing.

5 Contact breaker - examination, renovation and adjustment

1 Access to the contact breakers is obtained by removing the left-hand cover.
2 To adjust the contact breaker gap, rotate the crankshaft in an anti-clockwise direction until the contact breaker gap is at its maximum. The gap should be within the range 0.3 - 0.4 mm (0.012 - 0.016 in) and can be checked with feeler gauges. Repeat

the procedure with the other contact breaker.

GT125 only (Fig. 3.1)
3 To adjust the gap, loosen the locking screw (2) and rotate the plate (3) with a screwdriver in the slot provided. Check the gap with feeler gauges retighten (2) when correct. Always check the gap after retightening, since it may have altered. Repeat the procedure for the other contact breaker.

GT185 only (Fig. 3.2)
4 To adjust the gap, loosen the locating screw (2) and rotate the eccentric adjuster screw (3) with a screwdriver. Check the gap with feeler gauges and retighten when correct (2). Always check the gap after retightening, since it may have altered. Repeat the procedure for the other contact breaker.

All models
5 To remove each complete contact breaker assembly, disconnect the wire from it and remove the locking screw (2).
6 Remove the circlip from the contact breaker assembly and pull the movable contact off the pin (note the position of any shims that may be fitted).
7 Check the contact breaker points for pitting or burning. If this is only slight, it can be removed by the use of a needle file or an oilstone. If severe, or the contacts do not meet squarely, renew the contact breaker points assembly.
8 When reassembling, lightly grease the contact breaker pin with a graphite or molybdenum grease.
9 Soak the lubricating felt pad in hypoid oil and squeeze out the excess before refitting.
10 Reassemble in the reverse order of dismantling. Always recheck the accuracy of the ignition timing and adjust as necessary.

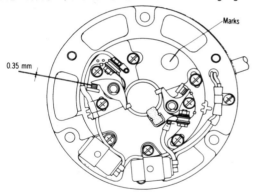

Fig. 3.1. Contact breaker assembly, GT125 model

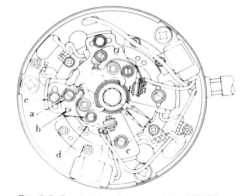

Fig. 3.2. Contact breaker assembly, GT185 model

5.2 Check the gap at its maximum opening

5.3a Slacken the screw and ...

5.3b ... adjust the gap, using a screwdriver in the slot provided

5.4 Turn this screw to adjust points gap (GT185 model)

5.9 Lubricate the felt oiler (arrowed)

6 Ignition timing - checking and adjustment

1   Ignition timing is very critical and to obtain maximum performance and trouble free running, it must be set accurately. Two methods are given below. The second (paragraph 4) is only an approximate method, which will suffice if no equipment is available. However, the much more accurate workshop method of timing is always to be preferred.

2   Check the ignition timing after having checked and set the contact breaker gaps; see previous Section.

3   Fit a dial test indicator (dti) into the spark plug hole of one cylinder. Connect a low wattage bulb (a 3.4W warning light bulb) between the contact breaker wire and earth. Turn the engine anti-clockwise until the correct ignition advance is shown on the dti, (see Specifications). Slacken the backing plate screws (6), turn on the ignition and rotate the backing plate until the bulb just goes out. This is the point when the contact breaker has just opened. Retighten the screws (6). Rotate the engine anti-clockwise a complete turn until the bulb just lights again and check that the reading on the dti. is within limits. Re-adjust as necessary. Turn off the ignition and repeat the procedure with the other cylinder and set of contact breaker points.

4   If only a rough check is required, rotate the crankshaft anti-clockwise and align the timing mark (4) for the right-hand cylinder with the index mark. In this position, the contact breaker points should just begin to open. The opening point can be checked with a 0.05 mm (0.0015 in) feeler gauge, which will just begin to go slack as the points open. Note that this is only an approximate check. If, in an emergency, a proper check cannot be carried out, a further check with a dial gauge must be made at the earliest possible opportunity.

5   To adjust the opening point, slacken the backing plate locking screws (6) and rotate the plate to obtain the correct opening point. Repeat the procedure with the other contact breaker, using the left-hand cylinder timing marks.

7 Spark plug - checking and resetting the gap

1   Both models are fitted with NGK spark plugs as standard. The GT125 and GT185 models both use NGK B8HS spark plugs. The plugs should be gapped within the range 0.6 - 0.7 mm (0.024 - 0.028 in). Certain operating conditions may indicate a change in spark plug grade, although the type recommended by the manufacturer will usually give the best, all round service. The use of anything other than the recommended grade may result in a holed piston.

2   Check the gap of the plug points during every three monthly or two thousand mile service. To reset the gap, bend the outer electrode to bring it closer to the centre electrode and check that the correct feeler gauge can be inserted. Never bend the central electrode or the insulator will crack, causing engine damage if the particles fall in whilst the engine is running.

3   With some experience, the condition of the spark plug electrode and insulator can be used as a reliable guide to engine operating conditions. See accompanying diagram.

4   Beware of overtightening the spark plugs otherwise there is risk of stripping the threads from the aluminium alloy cylinder head. Each plug should be sufficiently tight to sit firmly on its copper sealing washer, and no more. Use a spanner which is a good fit to prevent the spanner slipping and breaking the insulator.

5   If the threads in the cylinder head strip as a result of over-tightening the spark plug, it is possible to reclaim the head by use of a Helicoil thread insert. This is a cheap and convenient method of replacing the threads; most motorcycles dealers operate a service of this kind.

6   Make sure that the plug insulating caps are a good fit and have their rubber seals. They should also be kept clean to prevent tracking. The caps contain the suppressor that eliminates both radio and television interference.

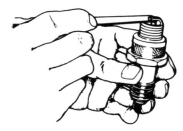 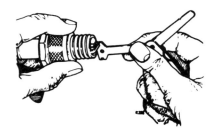

Fig. 3.3a. Spark plug maintenance

Checking plug gap with feeler gauges

Altering the plug gap. Note use of correct tool

Fig. 3.3b. Spark plug electrode condition

A *White deposits and damaged porcelain insulation indicating overheating*

B *Broken porcelain insulation due to bent central electrode*

C *Electrodes burnt away due to wrong heat value or chronic pre-ignition (pinking)*

D *Excessive black deposits caused by over-rich mixture or wrong heat value*

E *Mild white deposits and electrode burnt indicating too weak a fuel mixture*

F *Plug in sound condition with light greyish brown deposits*

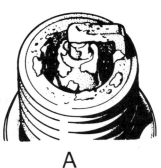  

A   B   C

D   E   F

6.3 Align the right-hand cylinder timing marks (emergency timing only)

6.4 Alignment of these marks gives rough check of ignition timing

8   Fault diagnosis - ignition system

Symptom	Cause	Remedy
Engine will not start	No spark at plugs	Faulty ignition switch. Check whether current is reaching ignition coil
	Weak spark at plugs	Dirty contact breaker points require cleaning Contact breaker gaps have closed up. Reset
Engine starts, but runs erratically	Intermittent or weak spark	Renew plugs. If no improvement check whether points are arcing. If so, replace condenser
	Ignition over-advanced	Check ignition timing and if necessary reset
	Plug lead insulation breaking down	Check for breaks in outer covering, especially near frame and plug caps
Engine difficult to start and runs sluggishly. Overheats	Ignition timing retarded	Check ignition timing and advance to correct setting

Chapter 4 Frame and forks

Contents

Specifications

							GT125	GT185
Lock (right and left) ...	...	...	...	...	...	...	42°	43°
Castor	...	...	...	...	...	...	63°	63°
Trail	...	...	...	...	...	...	87 mm (3.4 in)	102 mm (4.0 in)
Turning radius ...	...	...	...	...	...	...	2.0 m (78.7 in)	2.0 m (78.7 in)
Fork leg oil capacity (each)	...	...	...	...	...	...	125 cc (0.22 pt)	125 cc (0.22 pt)
'A' models only	...	...	...	...	...	...	125 cc (0.22 pt)	130 cc (0.23 pt) - L, M and A models

1 General description

1 The frame is a welded tubular structure having a single down tube but with top rails and a spine that triangulates the steering head. The front forks are of the telescopic type with internal springs; oil is used as the damping medium. The rear suspension units have external coil springs, these units are also damped with oil. The units are adjustable and have five different settings.

2 Front forks - removal and replacement

1 To remove the forks complete with the front wheel and bottom yoke, follow paragraphs 2 - 5 of this Section. If, however, it is necessary only to remove the fork legs, refer to paragraphs 6 - 9 of this Section.
2 Place the machine on its centre stand, so that it is standing firmly on level ground. Undo the hydraulic brake pipe on the bracket under the tachometer head. Be careful not to get any brake fluid on the paintwork. It is an excellent paint stripper. On the GT185K models only undo and remove the front brake cable.
3 Undo the speedometer drive cable and free the cable.
4 Remove the steering head column bolt. Slacken the two top yoke pinch bolts and lift off the top yoke.
5 Using a C-spanner, remove the large ring nut. The forks are now free and can be lowered out of the steering head. Be careful not to loose the ball bearings that will drop out as the bearing cups and cones separate. It will be necessary to raise the front end of the machine considerably so that the forks will clear the steering head.

6 Remove the front wheel as described in Chapter 5, Section 3.
7 Remove the front brake caliper by undoing the two retaining bolts.
8 Remove the mudguard which is held by four bolts.
9 Slacken both the pinch bolts in both the top and bottom yokes. The fork legs can now be withdrawn downwards.
10 Fork replacement is the reversal of the dismantling procedure. If the complete forks have been removed, the steering head bearings will also have to be replaced and adjusted; see Sections 5 and 6 respectively.
11 Do not forget to refill the fork legs with oil. Before tightening the bottom yoke fork pinch bolts, operate the forks several times to align the stanchions in the yokes. Tighten from the bottom upwards.

3 Front forks - dismantling, examination and renovation

1 Remove the stanchion top nut; note the rubber 'O'-ring seal.
2 Remove the spacer, spring seat and spring. Invert the fork leg and drain off the oil.
3 Pull off the rubber shroud from the fork slider.
4 Remove the Allen screw in the bottom of the slider and pull out the stanchion, complete with the damper assembly.
5 Remove the circlip from the end of the stanchion and withdraw the damper assembly.
6 The damper assembly can be stripped, if required, by the removal of the circlip and roll pin.
7 The oil seal in the slider can be prised out, after having first removed the wire circlip. Renew if in doubt, or if the fork leg was leaking oil.

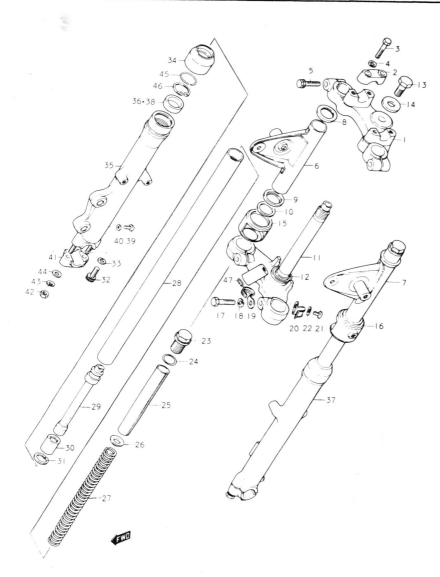

Fig. 4.1. Front forks

1 Top yoke
2 Handlebar clamp - 2 off
3 Bolt - 4 off
4 Spring washer - 4 off
5 Bolt - 2 off
6 Headlamp bracket, right-hand
7 Headlamp bracket, left-hand
8 Headlamp bracket top
   cover - 2 off
9 Headlamp bracket bottom
   cover - 2 off
10 Rubber bush - 2 off
11 Steering column and
    bottom yoke
12 Bottom race
13 Bolt
14 Washer
15 Reflector holder, right-hand
16 Reflector holder, left-hand
17 Bolt
18 Spring washer
19 Cable clip
20 Cable clip
21 Screw
22 Spring washer
23 Fork top bolt - 2 off
24 O-ring - 2 off
25 Spacer - 2 off
26 Spring seat - 2 off
27 Spring - 2 off
28 Stanchion - 2 off
29 Damper tube - 2 off
30 Piston - 2 off
31 Ring - 2 off
32 Allen screw - 2 off
33 Fibre washer - 2 off
34 Rubber shroud
35 Slider, right-hand
36 Oil seal
37 Slider, left-hand
38 Oil seal
39 Screw - 2 off
40 Fibre washer - 2 off
41 Spindle clamp - 2 off
42 Nut - 4 off
43 Spring washer - 4 off
44 Washer - 4 off
45 Wire circlip - 2 off
46 Circlip - 2 off
47 Wire circlip

8   The forks are not fitted with replaceable bushes; the chromed stanchion bears direct on the alloy slider. If play occurs, it is most likely that the slider will have worn. A secondary check can be made by inspecting the condition of the chrome plating on the stanchion.

9   If the fork action is 'sticky', check that the stanchion is not bent by either rolling it on a flat surface or by looking along it. If it is bent, a new stanchion will have to be obtained. It is not advisable to straighten a bent stanchion without the appropriate jigs.

10   Thoroughly clean off the components and reassemble them in the reverse order of dismantling. Do not forget to refill the fork legs with oil.

---

4 Fork leg oil - draining and refilling

1   Remove the drain screw in the fork legs and slacken the fork tube top nuts. Pump the forks to expell all the oil and replace the drain screws.

2   Remove the top bolts, one at a time, and refill each leg with the correct volume of oil (see Specifications). Replace and tighten the top bolts.

2.8 Remove the mudguard stay bolts

2.9a Slacken the top and ...

2.9b ... bottom yoke pinch bolts and ...

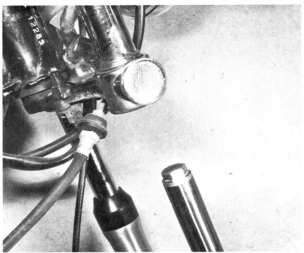

2.9c ... withdraw the fork leg downwards

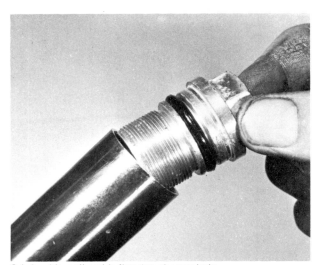

3.1 A rubber oil seal is fitted to the top bolt

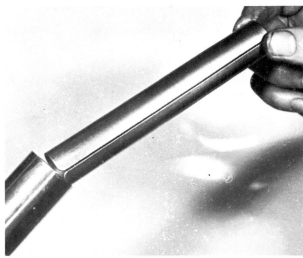

3.2a Lift out the spacer followed by ...

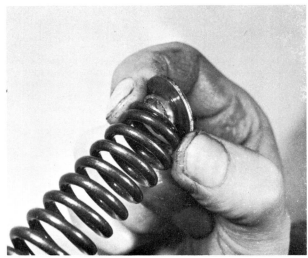

3.2b ... the spring seat and spring

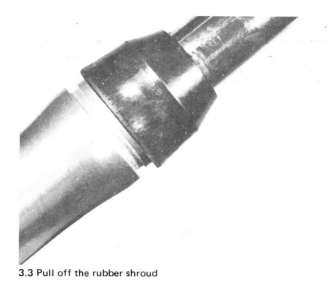

3.3 Pull off the rubber shroud

3.4 Unscrew the Allen screw

3.5a Remove the circlip and ...

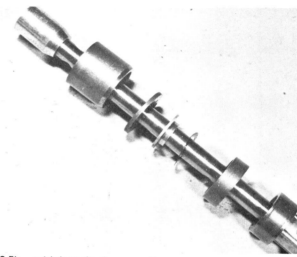

3.5b ... withdraw the damper unit

3.6a Remove the circlip and ...

3.6b ... roll pin

3.7a Remove the wire circlip to ...

3.7b ... gain access to the oil seal

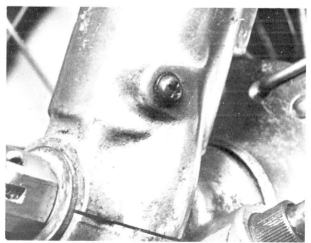

4.1 Drain the forks by removing this screw

5 Steering head lock - location and removal

1 The steering head lock is operated by the ignition key. Depending on the type of forks fitted, it is located either between the fork legs, underneath the head light, or on the right hand side of the bottom fork yoke.

2 The lock body of the centrally mounted lock is held in position by a circlip which, if removed, allows the lock action to be pulled out.

3 The lock body on the right-hand side mounted lock is held by two crosshead screws. Removal of the lock is effected by undoing the two screws. Replacement keys are available if the originals are lost.

6 Steering head bearings - examination and replacement

1 Before reassembly of the forks is commenced, examine the steering head races. The ball bearing tracks of the respective cup and cone bearings should be polished and free from indentations or cracks. If wear or damage is evident, the cups and cones must be renewed. They must be renewed as a complete set. With the exception of the upper steering head cone, the cups and cones are a tight press fit in their locations, and must be drifted out.

2 Ball bearings are inexpensive, therefore if the originals are marked or discoloured they should be renewed. To hold the steel balls in position during reassembly, pack the bearings with grease. Twenty two ball bearings are fitted to the upper race and eighteen to the lower. It will be found that with the correct number of ball bearings in each race, that there is space for the addition of one ball. This must be left free to prevent the balls skidding on one another, a situation that would greatly accelerate the rate of wear.

7 Steering head - adjustment

1 Slacken the steering head column bolt and the large nut underneath the top yoke.

2 Using a C-spanner, adjust the bearings by turning the large ring nut. Do not overtighten the bearings otherwise the handling characteristics of the machine will be affected. It is easily possible to overtighten and create a load of several tons on the bearing, although the handlebars will still appear to move with relative ease. This increase in load will greatly accelerate the wear of the bearings. As a guide, only very slight pressure should be needed to start the forks turning to either side under their own weight, when the front wheel is clear of the ground. Check also that the bearings are not to slack; there should be no discernable movement in the fore and aft direction.

3 Retighten the large nut whilst holding the ring nut with the C-spanner. Check that the adjustment has not altered; readjust again, if necessary. Finally, retighten the steering column stem bolt.

4 Loose steering head bearings will cause the forks to judder when the front brake is applied hard. Overtight bearings will give rise to a characteristic low speed roll, making it difficult to steer in a straight line.

8 Rear suspension units - removal, examination and setting

1 The rear suspension units are held by studs welded to the frame at the top on the swinging arm, at the bottom. To remove each unit, undo the two domed nuts and pull the unit off the studs. Note that six washers are fitted to each unit; three behind and three in front (except on the GT185K model, where only one washer is fitted on the front). Two types of suspension units have been fitted, the difference being the top shroud on the 'A' models.

2   The suspension units are sealed and there is no means of repairing them. If the damping fails or if the unit leaks, renewal is necessary.

3   In the interests of good roadholding it is essential that both suspension units have the same load setting. Also, if renewal is necessary, the units must be replaced as a pair.

4   The units can be adjusted using a small tommy bar or a screwdriver. Five settings are possible and a guideline is given below:

Position 1 (least tension)	*Normal running at moderate speeds without a pillion passenger*
Position 3 (middle setting)	*High speed touring, normal use*
Position 5 (greatest tension)	*High speed with a pillion passenger and/or heavy loads*

Adjustment is usually a question of personal preference

7.2 A C-spanner should be used on the ring nut

8.1 A domed nut is fitted to both top and bottom of suspension unit

9   Swinging arm rear fork - removal, renovation and replacement

1   After a lengthy period, the bushes in the swinging arm pivot bearing will wear, causing the roadholding to deteriorate and the machine twitch or hop. Under these circumstances, the bearings will have to be renewed. To detach the swinging arm, remove the rear wheel as described in Chapter 5, Section 13. Also remove the rear chain by undoing the connecting spring link. There is no necessity to remove the rear wheel sprocket.

2   Remove both the rear suspension units by undoing the four domed nuts and by pulling the units off their studs.

3   If required, the chainguard can be removed by undoing its two bolts; note the spacer fitted into the front lug, of the swinging arm.

4   Undo the pivot spindle nut and withdraw the spindle. Lift out the swinging arm. Note the plastic chain protector, fitted to the left-hand side.

GT125 models
5   Check the condition of the rubber bonded bushes and renew them, if necessary. Also check the pivot bolt for wear and straightness. Press out the old bushes with the new ones. A vice and a socket of a suitable diameter used as a spacer can be utilised for this purpose.

GT185 models
6   The GT185 is fitted with bushes and bearing collars. The bushes are lubricated by grease.

7   Slide out the collars and drift the bushes out from the opposite sides of the swinging arm. If there is play in the bushes, both bushes and collars must be renewed. Check also the condition of the dust seals and renew them, if necessary.

All models
8   To reassemble, reverse the dismantling procedure.

9   Do not tighten the pivot bolt nut until the swinging arm is in its normal working position (ie; with the suspension units connected) otherwise the bonded bushes will be placed under a permanent torque loading. This precaution is only applicable to the GT125 model. To lubricate the bushes on the GT185 model, pump grease into the grease nipple until it issues from both sides of the swinging arm.

10   Frame - examination and renovation

1   The frame is unlikely to require attention unless accident damage has occurred. In some cases, replacement of the frame is the only satisfactory course of action if it is badly out of alignment. Only a few frame repair specialists have the jigs and mandrels necessary for resetting the frame to the required standard of accuracy and even then there is no easy means of assessing to what extent the frame may have been overstressed.

2   After the machine has covered a considerable mileage, it is advisable to examine the frame closely for signs of cracking or splitting at the welded joints. Rust corrosion can also cause weakness at these joints. Minor damage can be repaired by welding or brazing, depending on the extent and nature of the damage.

3   Remember that a frame which is out of alignment will cause handling problems and may even promote 'speed wobbles'. If misalignment is suspected, as the result of an accident, it will be necessary to strip the machine completely so that the frame can be checked and, if necessary, renewed.

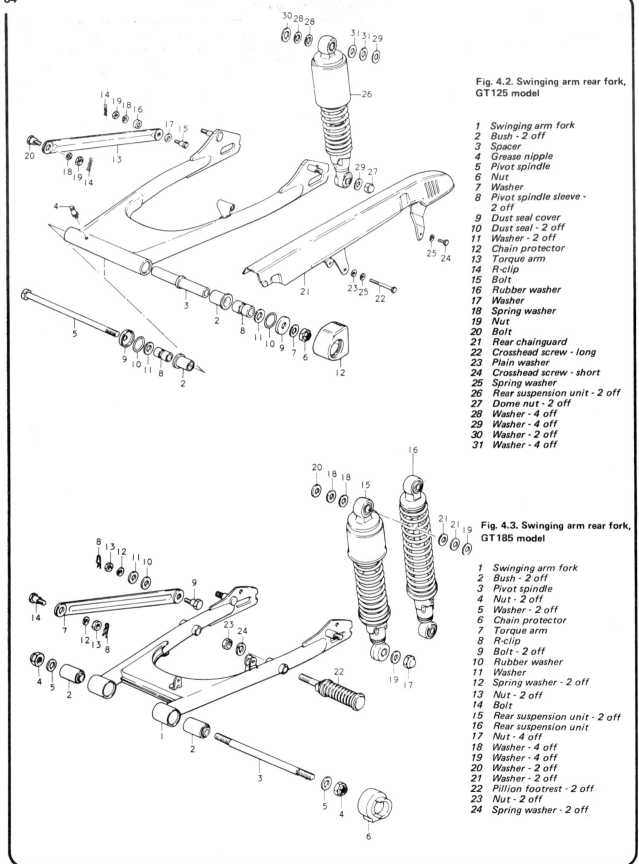

Fig. 4.2. Swinging arm rear fork, GT125 model

1   Swinging arm fork
2   Bush - 2 off
3   Spacer
4   Grease nipple
5   Pivot spindle
6   Nut
7   Washer
8   Pivot spindle sleeve - 2 off
9   Dust seal cover
10 Dust seal - 2 off
11 Washer - 2 off
12 Chain protector
13 Torque arm
14 R-clip
15 Bolt
16 Rubber washer
17 Washer
18 Spring washer
19 Nut
20 Bolt
21 Rear chainguard
22 Crosshead screw - long
23 Plain washer
24 Crosshead screw - short
25 Spring washer
26 Rear suspension unit - 2 off
27 Dome nut - 2 off
28 Washer - 4 off
29 Washer - 4 off
30 Washer - 2 off
31 Washer - 4 off

Fig. 4.3. Swinging arm rear fork, GT185 model

1   Swinging arm fork
2   Bush - 2 off
3   Pivot spindle
4   Nut - 2 off
5   Washer - 2 off
6   Chain protector
7   Torque arm
8   R-clip
9   Bolt - 2 off
10 Rubber washer
11 Washer
12 Spring washer - 2 off
13 Nut - 2 off
14 Bolt
15 Rear suspension unit - 2 off
16 Rear suspension unit
17 Nut - 4 off
18 Washer - 4 off
19 Washer - 4 off
20 Washer - 2 off
21 Washer - 2 off
22 Pillion footrest - 2 off
23 Nut - 2 off
24 Spring washer - 2 off

9.3a Remove the chainguard bolts

9.3b Note the spacer on the front mounting

9.4a Withdraw the pivot bolt and ...

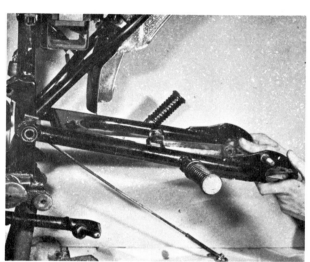

9.4b ... lift the swinging arm clear

9.4c A chain protector is fitted to the swinging arm

9.5 Bonded rubber bushes are fitted to the GT125 models

11 Footrests - renovation

1   If the footrests, have become bent, as may occur, if the machine has been dropped, they can be straightened by heating and bending.

2   Remove the footrest bar from the machine by undoing the two front bolts and slackening the two at the rear. Remove the footrest rubbers.

3   Heat the footrest bar, playing a blowlamp on the bent section whilst holding it in a vice and then bend it back to its original shape. Never attempt to straighten the bar whilst it is still attached to the machine, since this will place a severe strain on the mounting points.

4   To renew the rear footrest rubbers, remove the split pin and pull out the clevis pin. The old rubber can now be slid off.

11.4 Remove split pin to renew the rubber

12 Centre and prop stand - examination

1   The centre stand is attached to the lower part of the frame and provides a convenient means of parking the machine. A prop stand is also fitted to some machines, which provides a means for very quick parking and for use on sloping ground.

2   Both stands have return springs and the return action of each stand should be checked regularly. If either stand falls whilst the machine is in motion, it could catch in the ground and cause an accident. If in doubt, renew the springs. Make sure the pivot bolts are tight, unworn and well lubricated.

13 Dual seat - removal

1   The dual seat is hinged on two clevis pins, which are retained by two split pins. Removal of the seat is accomplished by removing the split pins and withdrawing the clevis pins.

14 Tachometer and speedometer cable - examination and renovation

1   It is advisable to detach the tachometer and speedometer drive cable from time to time, in order to check whether it is adequately lubricated and whether the outer covering is compressed or damaged at any point along its run. A jerky or sluggish speedometer movement can often be attributed to a cable fault.

2   To grease the cable, withdraw the inner cable. After removing the old grease, clean with a petrol soaked rag and examine the cable for broken strands or other damage.

3   Regrease the cable with high melting point grease, taking care not to grease the last six inches at the point where the cable enters the instrument head. If this precaution is not observed, grease will work into the head and immobilise the movement.

4   If both the speedometer head and the odometer stop working, it is probable that the speedometer cable is broken. Inspection will show whether the inner cable has broken. If so, the inner cable alone can be renewed and reinserted in the outer covering, after greasing. Never fit a new inner cable alone if the outer cover is damaged or compressed at any point along its run.

15 Cleaning the machine

1   After removing all surface dirt with a rag or sponge which is washed frequently in clean water, the machine should be allowed to dry thoroughly. Application of car polish or wax to the cycle parts will give a good finish, particularly if the machine receives this attention at regular intervals.

2   The plated parts should require only a wipe with a damp rag, but if they are badly corroded, as may occur during the winter when the roads are salted, it is permissible to use one of the proprietary chrome cleaners. These often have an oily base which will help to prevent corrosion from recurring.

3   If the engine parts are particularly oily, use a cleaning compound such as Gunk or Jizer. Apply the compound whilst the parts are dry and work it in with a brush so that it has an opportunity to penetrate and soak into the film of oil and grease. Finish off by washing down liberally, taking care that water does not enter the carburettor, air cleaner or the electrics. If desired, the now clean aluminium alloy parts can be enhanced still further when they are dry by using a special polish such as Solvol Autosol. This will restore the full lustre.

4   If possible, the machine should be wiped down immediately after it has been used in the wet, so that it is not garaged under damp conditions that will promote rusting. Make sure the chain is wiped and re-oiled, to prevent water from entering the rollers and causing harshness with an accompanying rapid rate of wear. Remember that there is less chance of water entering the control cables and causing stiffness if they are lubricated regularly as described in the Routine Maintenance Section.

16 Fault diagnosis -frame and forks

Symptom	Cause	Remedy
Machine veers either to the left or the right with hands off handlebars	Bent frame Twisted forks Wheels out of alignment	Check and renew. Check and renew. Check and re-align.
Machine rolls at low speed	Overtight steering head bearings	Slacken until adjustment is correct.
Machine judders when front brake is applied	Slack steering head bearings Worn fork legs	Tighten until adjustment is correct. Renew worn parts.
Machine pitches on uneven surfaces	Ineffective fork dampers Ineffective rear suspension units Suspension too soft	Check oil content. Check whether units still have damping action. Raise suspension unit adjustment one notch.
Fork action stiff	Fork legs out of alignment (twisted in yokes)	Slacken yoke clamps, and fork top bolts. Pump fork several times then retighten from bottom upwards.
Machine wanders. Steering imprecise. Rear wheel tends to hop	Worn swinging arm pivot	Dismantle and renew bushes and pivot shaft.

Chapter 5 Wheels, brakes and tyres

Contents

Specifications

Unless specific mention is made, the Specifications are the same for both the GT125 and GT185 models.

Brakes

Front brake diameter *GT185K model only	159.4 mm
Wear limit	154 mm
Disc thickness	5.00 mm
Wear limit	4.00 mm
Disc run out max.	0.1 mm
Wear limit	0.3 mm
Master cylinder bore diameter	14.00 - 14.04 mm
Wear limit	Greater than 14.05 mm
Master cylinder piston diameter	13.96 - 13.98 mm
Wear limit	Less than 13.94 mm
Caliper bore diameter	38.18 - 38.20 mm
Wear limit	38.15 - 38.18 mm
Rear brake diameter*	130 mm
Wear limit	130.7 mm

*measured with the shoes on the brake plate

Tyres

Front	2.75 x 18
Rear	3.00 x 18

1 General description

1 All the models utilise the same wheels and braking system except for the GT185K model whose front wheel differs due to the use of a twin leading shoe front brake.
2 A stainless steel disc is used for the hydraulically operated front brake, to prevent corrosion and increase the life of the disc.
3 A quickly detachable rear wheel is fitted, which allows removal without having to disturb the final drive chain and sprocket. A vane/rubber cush drive is fitted into the rear wheel to reduce the shock loading on the chain and to give a smoother ride.

2 Wheels - examination and renovation

1 Place the machine on blocks so that the wheel is raised clear of the ground. Spin the wheel, and by using a screwdriver as a pointer, check the rim alignment.
   Small irregularities can be corrected by tightening the spokes in the affected area, although a certain amount of experience is advisable to prevent over-correction. Any flats in the wheel rim should be evident at the same time. These are more difficult to remove and in most cases it will be necessary to have the wheel rebuilt on a new rim. Apart from the effect on stability, a flat will expose the tyre bead and walls to greater risk of damage if the machine is run with a deformed wheel.

2 Check for loose and broken spokes. Tapping the spokes is the best guide to tension. A loose spoke will produce a quite different sound and should be tightened by turning the nipple in an anti-clockwise direction. Always re-check for run-out by spinning the wheel again. If the spokes have to be tightened an excessive amount, it is advisable to remove the tyre and tube by following the procedure detailed in Section 19 of this Chapter. This is so that the protruding ends of the spokes can be ground off, to prevent them from chafing the inner tube and causing punctures.

3 Front wheel - removal and replacement

1 Place the machine on the centre stand, so that it is standing firmly on level ground. Place some packing under the front of the underside of the frame, so that the machine cannot topple forward when the front wheel is removed. Unscrew the speedometer cable nut and withdraw the cable.
2 Remove the split pin and undo the castellated nut.
3 Slacken the two cap retaining nuts on the bottom on the left hand fork slider and withdraw the wheel spindle. The wheel

complete with disc can now be removed; note that a spacer is fitted to both sides. As a precaution, place a wedge of wood in between the disc pads, to stop the inadvertant expulsion of the pad by touching the front brake lever.
4 Replacement is a reversal of the above. Before finally tightening up, operate both the brake and the front forks, to centralise the disc and wheel in the forks.

GT185K model only
5 Unclip the front brake cable. Remove the circlip and pull out the speedometer cable.
6 Slacken the two cap retaining nuts on the bottom of the right-hand fork slider. Undo and withdraw the wheel spindle. The wheel, complete with brake plate, can now be removed from the forks.
7 Replacement is a reversal of the above. Make sure to locate the brake plate over the anchor lug on the fork slider when replacing the wheel. Before tightening the wheel spindle, operate the brake to centralise the linings in the drum. Also, operate the forks a couple of times before tightening the two fork slider cap nuts. This will ensure that the wheel is centralised in the forks.

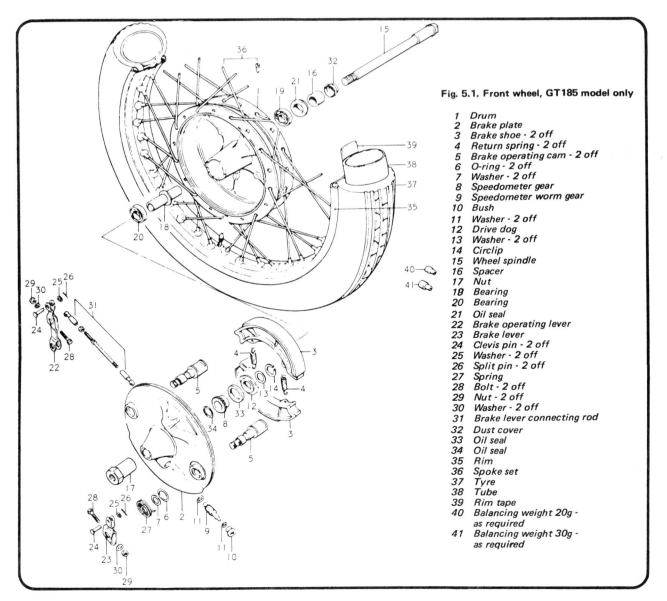

Fig. 5.1. Front wheel, GT185 model only

1 Drum
2 Brake plate
3 Brake shoe - 2 off
4 Return spring - 2 off
5 Brake operating cam - 2 off
6 O-ring - 2 off
7 Washer - 2 off
8 Speedometer gear
9 Speedometer worm gear
10 Bush
11 Washer - 2 off
12 Drive dog
13 Washer - 2 off
14 Circlip
15 Wheel spindle
16 Spacer
17 Nut
18 Bearing
20 Bearing
21 Oil seal
22 Brake operating lever
23 Brake lever
24 Clevis pin - 2 off
25 Washer - 2 off
26 Split pin - 2 off
27 Spring
28 Bolt - 2 off
29 Nut - 2 off
30 Washer - 2 off
31 Brake lever connecting rod
32 Dust cover
33 Oil seal
34 Oil seal
35 Rim
36 Spoke set
37 Tyre
38 Tube
39 Rim tape
40 Balancing weight 20g - as required
41 Balancing weight 30g - as required

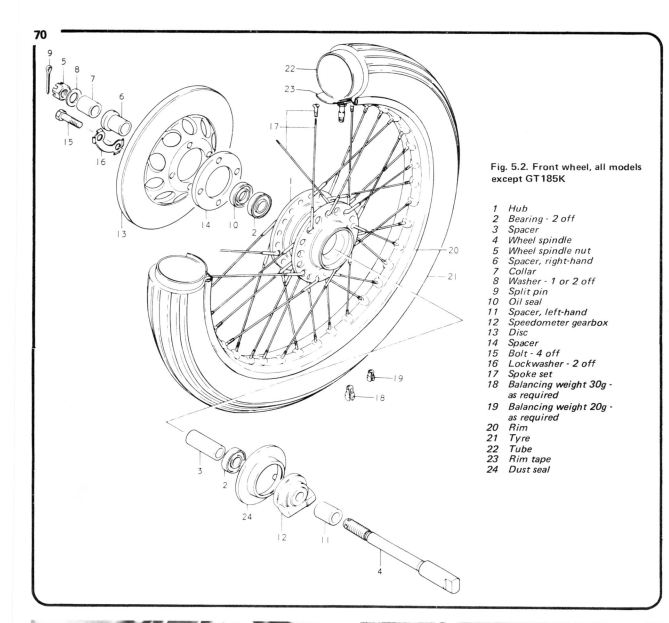

Fig. 5.2. Front wheel, all models except GT185K

1 Hub
2 Bearing - 2 off
3 Spacer
4 Wheel spindle
5 Wheel spindle nut
6 Spacer, right-hand
7 Collar
8 Washer - 1 or 2 off
9 Split pin
10 Oil seal
11 Spacer, left-hand
12 Speedometer gearbox
13 Disc
14 Spacer
15 Bolt - 4 off
16 Lockwasher - 2 off
17 Spoke set
18 Balancing weight 30g - as required
19 Balancing weight 20g - as required
20 Rim
21 Tyre
22 Tube
23 Rim tape
24 Dust seal

3.1 Remove the speedometer drive cable

3.3 A shouldered spacer is fitted on the disc side

4 Wheel bearings - removal and replacement

1   The ball journal wheel bearings are all fitted with integral oil seals, although an extra seal is located on the right-hand side of the front wheel.

2   The bearings are a drive fit in the hub and are removed by driving them out with a drift, working from each side of the hub. When the first bearing emerges from the hub, the hollow distance collar that separates the bearing can be removed.

3   Remove all the grease from the hub and bearings. Check the bearings for play or roughness when they are rotated. If there is any doubt about their condition renew them.

4   Before replacing the bearings, first pack the hub with a new high melting point grease, leaving sufficient room for expansion of the grease when it becomes hot. It is only necessary to pack the hub with grease if the bearings are not fitted with an oil seal either side. If they are sealed for life ie; two oil seals, no grease is necessary. Drift the bearing back into the hub using a tubular drift, contacting on only the outer ring of the bearing (an appropriate size socket will suffice). When the bearing has only one integral oil seal, make sure this is on the outside. Do not forget the distance collar between the bearings.

5   On the rear wheel a third bearing and an additional oil seal is contained in the sprocket carrier. Drift out the spindle and remove the spacer. Prise out the oil seal. The bearing can now be drifted out from the other side of the carrier. Check the bearing as before and again repack with high melting point grease. Refit as for the other wheel bearings. Replace the oil seal (renew if necessary), spacer and spindle.

5 Front disc hydraulic brake - general description

1   The hydraulic brake comprises five main components; the master cylinder for pressurising the system, the brake pipe to transmit the pressure and a caliper, which presses the friction pads onto the brake disc.

6 Front brake master cylinder - removal and renovation

1   Two different types of master cylinder have been used on the GT125 and GT185 models. The newer and current master cylinder is fitted to the M & A suffix models and has a piston pre-assembled with seals. The earlier master cylinder had separate, replaceable rubbers, which necessitates a complete strip down.

2   Before the master cylinder can be removed, the system must be drained. Place a clean container below the caliper unit and attach a plastic tube from the bleed screw on top of caliper unit to the container. Open the bleed screw one complete turn and drain the system by operating the brake lever until the master cylinder reservoir is empty. Close the bleed screw and remove the pipe.

3   Remove the front brake stop lamp switch from the master cylinder (USA and Canadian specification models). Unscrew the union bolt and disconnect the connection between the brake hose and the master cylinder. Unscrew the two master cylinder fastening bolts and remove the master cylinder body from the handlebar. Empty and surplus fluid from the reservoir.

4   Remove the brake lever from the body, remove the boot stopper, (taking care not to damage the boot) and then remove the boot. Remove the circlip that was hidden by the boot, the piston, primary cup, spring and check valve. Place the parts in a clean container and wash them in new brake fluid. Examine the cylinder bore and piston for scoring. Renew if scored. Check also the brake lever for pivot wear, cracks or fractures, the hose union threads and brake pipe threads for cracks or other signs of deterioration. If the appropriate measuring equipment is available measure the bore and piston diameter and compare with the Specifications.

5   When assembling the master cylinder follow the removal procedure in reverse order. Pay particular attention to the following points: Make sure the primary cup is fitted the correct way round. Renew the split pin of the brake lever pivot nut and fit it securely. Mount the master cylinder to the handlebar so the gap between it and the twist grip/switch unit is 2 mm (0.08 in) and the reservoir is horizontal when the motorcycle is on the centre stand with the steering in the straight ahead direction. Fill with fresh fluid and bleed the system. Be sure to check the brake reservoir by removing the reservoir cap. If the level is below the ring mark inside the reservoir, refill to the level with the prescribed brake fluid.

6   The component parts of the master cylinder assembly and the caliper assembly may wear or deteriorate in function over a long period of use. It is however generally difficult to forsee how long each component will work with proper efficiency and from a safety point of view it is best to change all the expendable parts every two years on a machine that has covered a normal mileage.

7   Note that any attention given to the master cylinder and its associated components must be carried out under clinically clean conditions. If any particles of dirt or grit enter the system, they will cause damage that will necessitate early renewal of the parts involved and perhaps initiate brake failure.

4.1 Remove the outer oil seal

4.2a Remove the front wheel bearing. Note the integral oil seal

4.2b Lift out the bearing spacer

4.2c Remove the rear wheel bearing. Note the integral oil seal ...

4.2d ... lift out the spacer

4.5a Drift out the spindle, ...

4.5b ... prise out the oil seal and ...

4.5c ... drift out the bearing

Fig. 5.3. Master cylinder

1   Piston cup assembly
2   Diaphragm
3   Diaphragm plate
4   Reservoir cup
5   Washer - 2 off
6   Bolt - 2 off
7   O-ring
8   Reservoir
9   Plate
10 Screw - 2 off

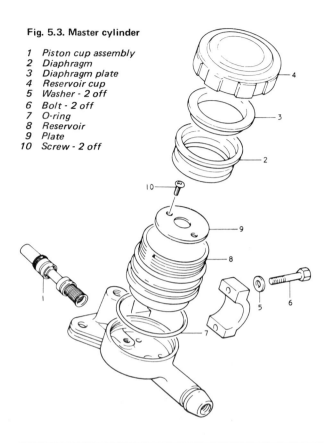

7.1 The wear limit is inscribed around the brake pad

8.1a Unscrew the caliper spindle bolts

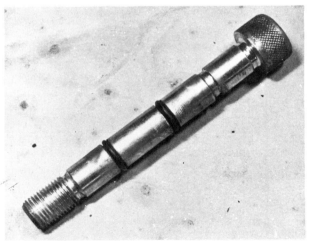

8.1b Both oil seals must be replaced

7   Front disc pads - examination and removal

1   Check the condition of the disc pads and if either is worn up to the red inscribed line on the circumference the pads must be renewed.

2   Remove the front wheel as described in Section 3 of this Chapter.

3   Unscrew the pad fastening screw from the fork leg. This is the single screw at the bottom. Take out the pad. The other pad is not secured with a screw and is ejected by squeezing the front brake lever two or three times. The pad will come out with fluid pressure. Apply Suzuki brake pad grease (which forms part of the brake pad set) onto the periphery and backplate of the second pad in a very thin layer. Push the pad back into the caliper body, and then mount the other pad in the caliper body, screwing in from the inside fork leg. Install the front wheel into the front forks, squeeze the brake lever two or three times to confirm its operation, and bleed air if necessary. (Refer to Section 9 if this Chapter if it is necessary to bleed air out of the system).

8   Front disc brake caliper - removal, examination and replacement

1   Unscrew the brake pipe nut from the caliper body. Undo the two bolts that hold the caliper body to the fork leg and pull the caliper body clear of the disc plate. Unscrew the caliper spindle bolts with an 8 mm Allen key; these are the two Allen screws on the top of the body. Separate the inner caliper body from the outer caliper body, remove the caliper holder and 'O' rings on the caliper spindles, then take out the caliper spindles and remove the piston boot. Push out the piston with compressed air whilst holding it with a finger to prevent it from blowing out.

Remove the piston seal with a small screwdriver inserted behind the seal. Wash the piston boot, piston seal and 'O' rings of the caliper in new brake fluid. Inspect the cylinder and the piston for wear which, if scored, will have to renewed. The rubber seals should also be renewed as the cost is very small, bearing in mind they could impair the efficiency of the brake.

CAUTION: Never use petrol for cleaning hydraulic brake parts otherwise the rubber components will be damaged. Do not wash the pads and also take care that brake fluid is not splashed onto them. Remember that hydraulic brake fluid is an excellent paint stripper and will also attack many plastic surfaces, especially instrument glasses.

2   If the appropriate measuring instruments are available, measure both the piston and bore and compare with the wear limits. Renew if necessary or without fail if either is badly scored.

3   To assemble the caliper, reverse the removal procedure. When assembling, pay attention to the following points. Apply Suzuki caliper grease (high heat resistance) to the caliper spindles. Apply a generous amount of brake fluid to the inner surface of the cylinder and to the periphery of the piston, then assemble. Do not assemble the piston with it inclined or twisted. When installing the piston, push it slowly into the cylinder while taking care not to damage the piston seal. Apply Suzuki brake pad grease around the periphery of the moving pad. Bleed the brake after refilling the reservoir with new hydraulic brake fluid then check for leakage while applying the brake lever tightly. After a test run, check the pads and brake disc.

4   Note that any work on the hydraulic system must be undertaken under ultra-clean conditions. Particles of dirt will score the working parts and cause early failure of the system.

9   Bleeding the front brake

1   If the brake lever travel has become excessive or the action 'spongy', the system probably has air in it and must be bled.
2   Fit a tube to the bleed nipple on the caliper.
3   Partially fill a clear container with a little brake fluid and immerse the end of the tube below the surface of the liquid. It must remain below the surface throughout the entire air bleeding operation.
4   Fill the master cylinder with brake fluid and replace the cap so as to prevent the entry of dust and/or fluid spurting out over the paintwork.
5   Rapidly operate the brake lever several times and with a little pressure still remaining on the lever, unscrew the bleed nipple a half turn. Squeeze the lever as far as possible and retighten the bleed nipple.
6   Repeat the procedure several times, until no more air bubbles appear. When bleeding, it is imperitive to keep the master cylinder topped up. If it should run dry and air enters the system, the entire operation will have to be started again.
7   Check the fluid level is between the marks, refit the diaphragm plate and tighten the cap.
8   Remove the tube and fit the dust cap.
9   Always use the correct grade hydraulic fluid and do not re-use the fluid that has been bleed from the system. It contains minute air bubbles and must stand for at least 24 hours so that they can disperse.

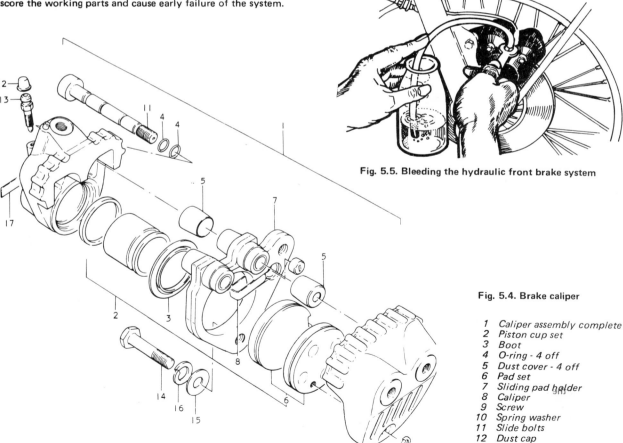

Fig. 5.5. Bleeding the hydraulic front brake system

Fig. 5.4. Brake caliper

1   *Caliper assembly complete*
2   *Piston cup set*
3   *Boot*
4   *O-ring - 4 off*
5   *Dust cover - 4 off*
6   *Pad set*
7   *Sliding pad holder*
8   *Caliper*
9   *Screw*
10 *Spring washer*
11 *Slide bolts*
12 *Dust cap*
13 *Bleed screw*
14 *Bolt - 2 off*
15 *Spring washer - 2 off*
16 *Spring washer - 2 off*
17 *Motif*

10 Front brake disc - checking and removal

1   The brake disc should only require removal if badly scored, warped, or if worn thin after long service.

2   The disc run-out is checked with the wheel in the forks. A dial test indicator should be adjusted to measure the run-out on the periphery of the disc. Compare with the limits and renew if necessary.

3   Measure the thickness of the disc, where it has been worn by the pads, using a micrometer. Compare with the limits and renew if necessary.

4   To remove the disc, first detach the front wheel as described in Section 3 of this Chapter. Knock back the tabs of the lock washer and remove the four nuts.

5   Replacement is a reversal of the above. Do not forget to fit the spacer behind the disc (L models only) to knock over the tabs of the lockwashers, after the nuts have been tightened fully.

9.2 Connect a bleed tube to the bleed nipple

10.5 Do not forget to knock over the tabs of the lockwasher

11 Adjusting the twin leading shoe front brake

GT185K model only

1   If the front brake adjustment is correct there should be a clearance of not less than 20 - 30 mm (0.8 - 1.2 in) between the brake lever and handlebars when the brake is applied fully.

2   Adjustment is effected by turning the adjuster nut in the end of the handlebar lever outwards to decrease the clearance or inwards to increase the clearance. If the adjuster on the brake plate is used instead, this will have the same effect.

3   The only time the operating rod connecting the two operating levers requires adjustment is when the original setting has been disturbed. It is imperative that the leading edge of each brake shoe contacts the brake drum at the same time for maximum braking efficiency.

4   Check by detaching the clevis pin from the eye of one end of the operating rod so that the brake operating arms can be applied independantly. Operate each arm separately and note when the brake shoe first makes contact with the brake drum surface. Make a mark to show the exact position of each operating arm when the initial contact is made. Replace the clevis pin and check that the marks coincide when the brake is applied in similar fashion. If they do not, withdraw the clevis pin and use the rod adjuster to extend or reduce the length of the operating rod until the marks correspond exactly. Replace the clevis pin and do not omit to insert the split pin through the end which retains the clevis pin in position. Recheck the brake lever adjustment before taking the machine on the road. As a rough guide the two brake operating arms should be parallel with one another when adjustment is correct.

5   Check that the brake pulls off correctly when the handlebar lever is released. Sluggish action can be due to a poorly lubricated cable or one with a frayed inner.

12 Speedometer drive gearbox - dismantling and renovation

All models except GT185K

1   The speedometer drive gearbox is located on the left-hand side of the front hub. To obtain access, the front wheel has to be removed as described in Section 3 of this Chapter.

2   The gearbox can be stripped for regreasing by removing the circlip; followed by the thrust washer, drive god, oil seal and gear.

3   The worm gear is removed by unscrewing the fibre sleeve nut. The worm can then be pulled out. Note that a thrust washer is fitted to both ends of the worm.

4   Clean the gears and lightly regrease them, using a high melting point grease. Check that the seal is in good condition and reassemble the gearbox.

GT185K model only

5   The speedometer drive gearbox is contained in the brake plate of the front wheel. Removal of the front wheel is required to gain access; see Section 3 of this Chapter.

6   Remove the circlip; followed by the thrust washer, drive dog and gear. Two oil seals are fitted, one either side of the gearbox. Check that they are in good condition - particularly the inner large seal since if this is faulty it will allow grease on to the brake linings.

7   The worm gear is retained by a bush in the brake plate. Note that a thrust washer is fitted to each end.

8   Clean the gears and lightly regrease them with a high melting point grease. Reassembly is a reversal of the above.

12.2a Remove the circlip followed by ...

12.2b ... the thrust washer and drive dog ...

12.2c ... leaving the oil seal in the gearbox

12.3a Unscrew the fibre sleeve and ...

12.3b ... withdraw the driveshaft. Note the two thrust washers

13 Rear wheel and brake - removal and replacement

1   The same pattern quickly detachable rear wheel is fitted to both the GT125 and GT185 models. This type of wheel makes it unnecessary to detach the final drive chain when it has to be removed.

2   Place the machine on its centre stand, so that it is standing firmly on level ground. Undo the brake rod adjuster and depress the brake pedal to remove the rod from the trunnion. Do not lose the spring or trunnion.

3   Remove the R-clip and nut on the brake end of the torque arm and free the arm from the brake plate.

4   Remove the split pin and undo the outer (smaller) wheel spindle nut. Withdraw the wheel spindle, complete with the chain adjuster. Note the spacer fitted on the right-hand side. Lift out the brake plate and shoes.

5   Pull the wheel towards the right-hand side, to free the cush drive and lift the wheel out by tilting the machine to the left, to obtain clearance.

6   Replacement is the reverse of the removal procedure. Do not forget to tighten the torque arm nut and to replace the R-clip. It may also be necessary to re-adjust the rear brake. Before tightening the wheel spindle nut, spin the wheel and apply the brake to centralise the brake shoes in the drum. Use a new split pin when the wheel nut has been tightened.

13.2 Remove the brake rod adjuster

13.3a Remove the R-clip and ...

13.3b ... and the torque arm nut and washer

13.4a Withdraw the wheel spindle and ...

13.4b ... lift out the brake plate

13.5 Free the wheel from the cush drive

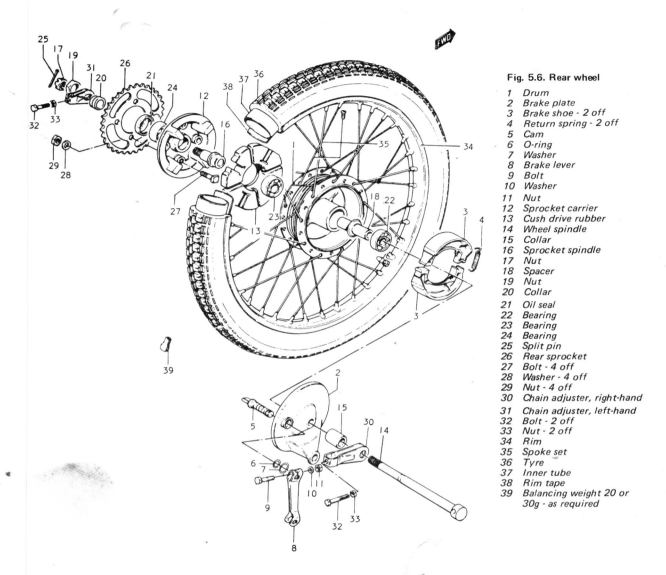

Fig. 5.6. Rear wheel

1   Drum
2   Brake plate
3   Brake shoe - 2 off
4   Return spring - 2 off
5   Cam
6   O-ring
7   Washer
8   Brake lever
9   Bolt
10 Washer
11 Nut
12 Sprocket carrier
13 Cush drive rubber
14 Wheel spindle
15 Collar
16 Sprocket spindle
17 Nut
18 Spacer
19 Nut
20 Collar
21 Oil seal
22 Bearing
23 Bearing
24 Bearing
25 Split pin
26 Rear sprocket
27 Bolt - 4 off
28 Washer - 4 off
29 Nut - 4 off
30 Chain adjuster, right-hand
31 Chain adjuster, left-hand
32 Bolt - 2 off
33 Nut - 2 off
34 Rim
35 Spoke set
36 Tyre
37 Inner tube
38 Rim tape
39 Balancing weight 20 or
    30g - as required

14 Drum brakes - dismantling, examination and replacement

1   The rear drum brake is common to all the models. Only the
GT185K model is fitted with the twin leading shoe front brake.
For servicing purposes the two types can be treated alike.
2   Remove the wheel and brake as described in Section 3 for the
front wheel of Section 13 for the rear wheel. Note that in the case
of the rear brake it is not necessary to remove the rear wheel
completely, only to proceed as far as withdrawing the wheel
spindle and removing the spacer. This then provides sufficient
clearance to remove the brake plate and brake shoes.
3   Examine the condition of the brake linings. If they are
wearing thin or unevenly the brake shoes should be renewed.
The linings are bonded to the brake shoes and cannot be supplied
separately. Measure the drum diameter and compare with the
Specifications.
4   To remove the brake shoes, pull them away from the brake
plate in a 'V' formation so that they can be lifted away together
with the return springs. When they are well clear of the brake
plate, the return springs can be disconnected.

5   Before replacing the brake shoes, check that the operating
cam is working smoothly and not binding in its housing. The
cam can be removed for greasing by detaching the operating arm
from the end of the shaft. The operating arm is located on the
cam shaft by splines, and is retained by a pinch bolt, mark both
the operating arm and the shaft end before removal to aid
correct relocation.
6   Check the inner surface of the brake drum, on which the
brake shoes bear. The surface should be free from indentations
and score marks, otherwise reduced braking efficiency and
accelerated brake lining wear will result. Remove all traces of
brake lining dust and wipe the drum surface with a petrol
soaked rag, to remove all traces of grease and oil.
7   To reassemble the brake shoes on the brake plate, fit the
return springs and pull the shoes apart whilst holding them in
the form of a 'V' facing upwards. If they are now located with
the brake operating cam and fixed pivot, they can be pushed
into position by pressing downwards. Do not use excessive force,
or there is risk of distorting the shoes. **Note:** A wear limit is
stamped on the brake drum and a wear indicator mark is cast on
the brake plate.

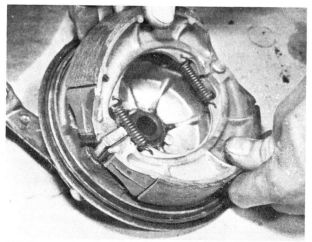

14.4 Remove the shoes by pulling them up into a Vee

14.7 The drum diameter is stamped in the drum

15 Adjusting the rear brake

1   If the adjustment of the rear brake is correct, the brake pedal
will have to travel up from 20 - 30 mm (0.8 - 1.2 in).
Before the amount of travel is adjusted, the brake pedal position
should be set so that the pedal is in the best position for quick
operation.
2   The height of the brake pedal is determined by the adjuster
at the end of the brake cable, where it joins the pedal arm. If the
adjuster is screwed inwards, the pedal height is raised and vice
versa.
3   The length of travel is controlled by the adjuster at the end
of the brake operating arm. If the nut is screwed inwards, travel
is decreased and vice versa.
4   Note that it may be necessary to readjust the height of the
stop lamp switch if the pedal height has been altered to any
marked extent. (See Chapter 6, Section 10).
5   A wear indicator mark is cast on the brake plate, so that the
amount of lining wear can be ascertained without need to remove
the brake itself.

16 Cush drive assembly - examination and replacement

1   The cush drive assembly is contained within the left-hand
side of the rear wheel hub. It comprises of a synthetic rubber
buffer assembly housed within a series of vanes cast in the hub
shell. A plate attached to the rear wheel sprocket has four
cast-in dogs that engage with slots in the rubbers. The drive to
the rear wheel is transmitted through the rubbers, which
cushion any surges and roughness in the drive which would
otherwise convey the impression of harshness.
2   Under normal riding conditions the cush drive rubber will
continue to be serviceable for an extended length of service. The
rubber should be tested in situ by firmly holding the rear wheel
and turning the sprocket alternately in a clockwise and anti-
clockwise direction. If it is evident that the rubber has become
permanently compressed it should be renewed.
3   The cush drive rubber is a push fit in the rear wheel hub and
thus present no problems to renew.

17 Rear wheel sprocket - removal, examination and replacement

1   The rear wheel sprocket can be removed as a separate unit
after the rear wheel has been detached from the frame as
described in Section 13 of this Chapter. The sprocket is retained

to the cush drive plate by four nuts and two lockwashers. The
tabs on the lockwasher must be knocked down before the nuts
can be loosened.
2   Check the condition of the sprocket teeth. If they are hooked,
chipped or badly worn the sprocket must be renewed. It is
considered bad practice to renew one sprocket on its own. The
final drive sprockets should always be renewed as a pair and a
new chain fitted, otherwise rapid wear will necessitate even
earlier replacement on the next occasion.
3   For bearing replacement, refer to Section 4, of this Chapter.

18 Final drive chain - examination, adjustment and lubrication

1   The final drive chain is exposed and periodically the tension
will need to be readjusted, to compensate for wear. This is
accomplished by slackening the rear wheel nuts after the
machine has been placed on the centre stand and drawing the
wheel backwards by means of the drawbolt adjusters in the fork
ends. The torque arm bolt on the rear brake plate must also be
slackened during this operation.
2   The chain is in correct tension if there is from 15 - 20 mm
(0.6 - 0.8 in.) of slack. Always check when the chain is at its
tightest point; a chain rarely wears evenly during service.
3   Always adjust the drawbolts an equal amount in order to
preserve wheel alignment. The fork ends are marked with a
series of horizontal lines above the adjusters, to provide a visual
check. If desired, wheel alignment can be checked by running a
plank of wood parallel to the machine, so that it touches both
walls of the rear tyre. If wheel alignment is correct, it should be
equi-distant from either side of the front wheel tyre, when tested
on both sides of the rear wheel. It will not touch the front wheel
tyre because this tyre is of smaller cross section. See accompanying diagram.
4   Do not run the chain overtight to compensate for uneven
wear. A tight chain will place excessive stresses on the gearbox
and rear wheel bearings, leading to their early failure. It will also
absorb a surprising amount of power.
5   After a period of running, the chain will require lubrication.
Lack of oil will accelerate wear of both chain and sprockets and
lead to harsh transmission. The application of engine oil will act
as a temporary expedient, but it is preferable to remove the chain
and immerse it in a molten lubricant such as 'Linklyfe' or
'Chainguard', after it has been cleaned in a paraffin bath. These
latter lubricants achieve better penetration of the chain links and
rollers and are less likely to be thrown off when the chain is in
motion.

6   To check whether the chain requires replacement, lay it lengthwise in a straight line and compress it endwise until all the play is taken up. Anchor one end and pull on the other in order to take up the end play in the opposite direction. If the chain extends by more than the distance between two adjacent rollers, it should be replaced in conjunction with the sprockets. Note that this check should be made **after** the chain has been washed out, but before any lubricant is applied, otherwise the lubricant will take up some of the play.

7   When replacing the chain, make sure the spring link is seated correctly, with the closed end facing the direction of travel.

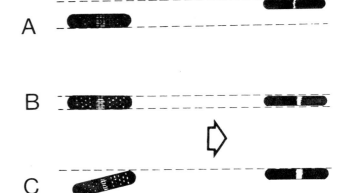

Fig. 5.7. Checking wheel alignment

A & C   Incorrect
B   Correct

16.3 The cush drive rubber is a push fit in the drum

17.1a Remove the sprocket carrier

17.1b Do not forget to bend over the tabs of the lockwasher

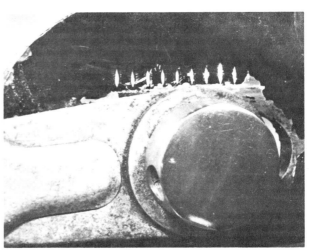

18.3 Make sure both adjusters are set on the same mark

19 Tyres - removal and replacement

1   At some time or other the need will arise to remove and replace the tyres, either as the result of a puncture or because a renewal is required to offset wear. To the inexperienced, tyre changing represents a formidable task yet if a few simple rules are observed and the technique learned, the whole operation is surprisingly simple.

2   To remove the tyre from the wheel, first detach the wheel from the machine. Deflate the tyre by removing the valve insert and when it is fully deflated, push the bead from the tyre away from the wheel rim on both sides so that the bead enters the centre well of the rim. Remove the locking cap and push the tyre valve into the tyre itself.

3   Insert a tyre lever close to the valve and lever the edge of the tyre over the outside of the wheel rim. Very little force should be necessary; if resistance is encountered it is probably due to the fact that the tyre beads have not entered the well of the wheel rim all the way round the tyre.

4   Once the tyre has been edged over the wheel rim, it is easy to work around the wheel rim so that the tyre is completely free on one side. At this stage, the inner tube can be removed.

5   Working from the other side of the wheel, ease the other edge of the tyre over the outside of the wheel rim that is furthest away. Continue to work around the rim until the tyre is free completely from the rim.

6   If a puncture has necessitated the removal of the tyre, reinflate the inner tube and immerse it in a bowl of water to trace the source of the leak. Mark its position and deflate the tube. Dry the tube and clean the area around the puncture with a petrol soaked rag. When the surface has dried, apply rubber solution and allow this to dry before removing the backing from the patch and applying the patch to the surface.

7   It is best to use a patch of self-vulcanising type, which will form a very permanent repair. Note that it may be necessary to remove a protective covering from the top surface of the patch, after it has sealed in position. Inner tubes made from synthetic rubber may require a special type of patch and adhesive, if a satisfactory bond is to be achieved.

8   Before replacing the tyre, check the inside to make sure the agent that caused the puncture is not trapped. Check the outside of the tyre, particularly the tread area, to make sure nothing is trapped that may cause a further puncture.

9   If the inner tube has been patched on a number of past occasions, or if there is a tear or large hole, it is preferable to discard it and fit a replacement. Sudden deflation may cause an accident, particularly if it occurs with the front wheel.

10   To replace the tyre, inflate the inner tube sufficiently for it to assume a circulat shape but only just. Then push it into the tyre so that it is enclosed completely. Lay the tyre on the wheel at an angle and insert the valve through the rim tape and the hole in the wheel rim. Attach the locking cap on the first few threads, sufficient to hold the valve captive in its correct location.

11   Starting at the point furthest from the valve, push the tyre bead over the edge of the wheel rim until it is located in the central well. Continue to work around the tyre in this fashion until the whole of one side of the tyre is on the rim. It may be necessary to use a tyre lever during the final stages.

12   Make sure there is no pull on the tyre valve and again commencing with the area furthest from the valve, ease the other bead of the tyre over the edge of the rim. Finish with the area close to the valve, pushing the valve up into the tyre until the locking cap touches the rim. This will ensure the inner tube is not trapped when the last section of the bead is edged over the rim with a tyre lever.

13   Check that the inner tube is not trapped at any point. Reinflate the inner tube, and check that the tyre is seating correctly around the wheel rim. There should be a thin rib moulded around the wall of the tyre on both sides, which should be equidistant from the wheel rim at all points. If the tyre is unevenly located on the rim, try bouncing the wheel when the tyre is at the recommended pressure. It is probable that one of the beads has not pulled clear of the centre well.

14   Always run the tyres at the recommended pressures and never under or over-inflate. The correct pressures for solo use are given in the Specification Section of this Chapter.

15   Tyre replacement is aided by dusting the side walls, particularly in the vicinity of the beads, with a liberal coating of french chalk. Washing-up liquid can also be used to good effect, but this has the disadvantage of causing the inner surfaces of the wheel rim to rust.

16   Never replace the inner tube and tyre without the rim tape in position. If this precaution is overlooked there is good chance of the ends of the spoke nipples chafing the inner tube and causing a crop of punctures.

17   Never fit a tyre that has a damaged tread or side walls. Apart from the legal aspects, there is a very great risk of a blow-out, which can have serious consequences on any two-wheel vehicle.

18   Tyre valves rarely give trouble, but it is always advisable to check whether the valve itself is leaking before removing the tyre. Do not forget to fit the dust cap, which forms an effective second seal.

20 Tyre valve dust caps

1   Tyre valve dust caps are often left off when a tyre has been replaced, despite the fact that they serve an important two-fold function. Firstly, they prevent dirt or other foreign matter from entering the valve and causing the valve to stick open when the tyre pump is next applied. Secondly, they form an effective second seal so that in the event of the tyre valve leaking, air will not be lost.

21 Wheel balance

1   On any high performance machine it is important that the front wheel is balanced, to offset the weight of the tyre valve. If this precaution is not observed, the out-of-balance wheel will produce an unpleasant hammering that is felt through the handlebars at speeds from approximately 50 mph upwards.

2   To balance the front wheel, place the machine on the centre stand so that the front wheel is well clear of the ground and check that it will revolve quite freely, without the brake shoes rubbing. In the unbalanced state, it will be found that the wheel always comes to rest in the same position, with the tyre valve in the six o'clock position. Add balance weights to the spokes diametrically opposite the tyre valve until the tyre valve is counterbalanced, then spin the wheel to check that it will come to rest in a random position on each occasion. Add or subtract weight until perfect balance is achieved.

3   Only the front wheel requires attention. There is little point in balancing the rear wheel because it will have little noticeable effect on road holding and general handling.

22 Fault diagnosis - wheels, brakes and tyres

Symptom	Cause	Remedy
Handlebars oscillate at low speeds	Buckled front wheel Incorrectly fitted front tyre	Remove wheel for specialist attention Check whether line around bead is equi-distant from rim.
Forks 'hammer' at high speeds	Front wheel out of balance	Add weights until wheel will stop in any position
Brakes grab, locking wheel	Ends of brake shoes not chamfered (drum brake)	Remove brake shoes and chamfer ends
Brakes feel spongy	Stretched brake operating cables, weak pull-off springs Air in hydraulic system (disc brake)	Replace cable and/or springs, after inspection Bleed system
Tyres wear more rapidly in middle of tread	Over-inflation	Check pressures and run at recommended settings
Tyres wear rapidly at outer edge of tread	Under-inflation	Ditto.
Harsh transmission	Worn or badly adjusted chains Hooked or badly worn sprockets	Adjust or replace as necessary Renew as a pair, together with chain

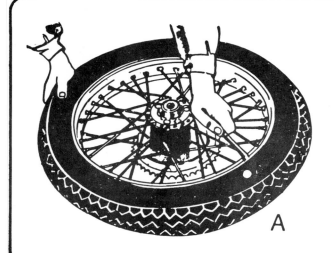

Fig. 5.8a. Tyre removal

A Deflate inner tube and insert lever in close proximity to tyre valve
B Use two levers to work bead over the edge of rim
C When first bead is clear of rim, remove tyre as shown

Fig. 5.8b. Tyre replacement

D *Inflate inner tube and insert in tyre*
E *Lay tyre on rim and feed valve through hole in rim*
F *Work first bead over rim, using lever in final section*
G *Use similar technique for second bead. Finish at tyre valve position*
H *Push valve and tube up into tyre when fitting final section, to avoid trapping*

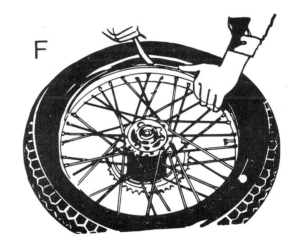

Chapter 6 Electrical system

Contents

Specifications

Unless specific mention is made, the Specifications are the same for both the GT125 and GT185 models; also all the electrical fittings are 12 volt

Battery ... ...   5 AH (GT125)   11 AH (GT185)

Fuse   ... ...   15 Amp

Bulbs
Headlight	35/25W
Rear/stop light	5/21 or 8/23 both models
Indicator warning light	1.7W
All other warning lights and instrument lights	3.4W
Flashing indicator lights	23W

Voltage regulator GT185 model only
No load voltage	15.4 - 16.6V @ 3000 rpm or greater
Cut in voltage	12.0 - 13.5V

1 General description

1 Both the GT125 and GT185 models share similar electrical fittings ie; switches, bulbs etc. Both models use a 12 volt negative earth system. However, the similarity ends there since on the GT125's an alternator (AC) and a silicon diode provide the electrical current while the GT185 models have a combined dynamo (DC)/starter motor and an associated voltage regulator and solenoid.

2 On both the GT125 and 185 models, the electrical system is protected by a fuse in the battery positive line.

2 Fuse - location and replacement

1 A 15 amp fuse in a plastic case is located in the battery positive lead and is clipped under the junction conector. The fuse gives protection from sudden overload, ie; a short circuit.

2 If a fuse blows, the electrical circuit should be checked for a fault before replacing it with another.

3 Always carry at least one spare fuse. This will get you home in an emergency, provided the reason for the original failure has been traced and remedied. Never use a fuse of a higher rating or its protective function will be lost.

4 When a fuse blows whilst the machine is running and no spare fuse is available, a get you home remedy is to remove the blown fuse and to wrap it in silver paper. This will restore electrical continuity by bridging the broken wire within the fuse. This expedient should **never** be used if there is evidence of a short circuit or other major electrical fault, otherwise more serious damage will be caused. Replace the temporary fuse at the earliest possible opportunity, to restore full circuit protection.

3 Battery - examination and maintenance

1 The electrolyte level of the battery should be maintained between the upper and lower limits marked on the case by topping up with distilled water (unless spillage has occured when it should be topped up with acid of the correct specific gravity). If, when the battery is in a fully charged condition (corresponding to approximately 12.12 volts) the specific gravity lies much below 1.26 - 1.28 at 20°C, the electrolyte should be replaced by fresh sulphuric acid of the correct specific gravity (1.26 - 1.28 at 20°C).

2   If the machine is not be used for a while, the battery
should be recharged every six weeks or so. If the battery is left
in a discharged condition for any length of time the plates will
sulphate and render it inoperative.

3   A normal charging rate of 0.4 amp should be used when
charging the battery off the machine.

4   If the battery case is cracked or leaking, a replacement
battery should be obtained, since it is not often that an
effective repair can be made. A leaking battery should never be
used, since the acid will severely corrode the cycle parts. If any
acid is spilt over the machine or rider, it should be washed off
immediately, with plenty of water.

4   Silicon rectifier - checking (GT125 model only)

1   Check for conduction, with a testmeter, between the
yellow/green and red leads in both directions. If the rectifier
either conducts in both directions, or not at all, it is faulty and
must be renewed. It is not repairable.

2   The rectifier is located behind the junction connector fuse
bracket.

5   Voltage regulator - checking (GT185 model only)

1   Disconnect the red lead from the regulator to the battery
and connect this wire to earth, via a voltmeter (see Fig. 6.1).
Start the engine and gradually increase engine speed. The
voltmeter should read a no load voltage of 15.4 - 16.6V at an
engine speed greater than 3000 rpm. If the meter reads over
16.6V or no voltage at all, the regulator is malfunctioning,
possibly due to burnt points. It will require attention by a
Suzuki agent.

2   The cut-in voltage is the voltage at which the points close and
the battery begins to charge. It should lie in the range 12.0 -
13.5V. To measure this, use one of the three circuits given in
Fig. 6.2. Do not measure the voltage when engine speed is
decreasing since low values will be obtained. In circuit (a),
measure the voltage when the current commences to flow
through the ammeter; in (b), as the lamp lights and in (c),
when the voltmeter needle shakes and stops ie; as the points
close.

2.1 The fuse is located behind the right hand panel

3.1 Electrolyte must be kept between the two levels

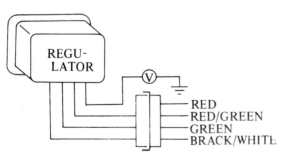

Fig. 6.1. Checking the voltage regulator, voltage control

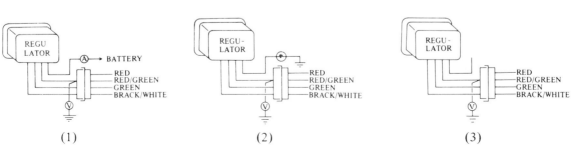

(1)   (2)   (3)

Fig. 6.2. Checking the voltage regulator, cut-in voltage

6 Dynamo - checking and servicing (GT185 model only)

1 Field coils continuity. Check the dynamo field coil for continuity with a testmeter connected between the red/green tracer and green leads (approx 4 - 6 ohms resistance). Connect the meter between the red/green tracer and yellow lead, to check the stator field coil. If either coils are open circuit, the windings are defective.

2 Field coil to earth insulation. Check between earth and the red/green tracer lead. There should be no conductance.

3 Armature to earth insulation. Check the insulation between each commutator strip and earth; there should be conductance. (It is not possible to check individual windings with a simple testmeter).

4 Carbon brushes. Measure the length of each brush and renew if it is under 14 mm (0.55 in).

5 Commutator. The commutator must be kept clean to obtain consistent starting and charging. Clean with fine emery paper (400 grit). Be careful to remove all the grit after cleaning. If the commutator is badly worn, it can be skimmed in a lathe up to a maximum of 1 mm (0.40 in) and then undercut to 0.5 mm (0.02 in). The commutator undercuts often become clogged with brush particles which should be cleaned out with a hacksaw blade of the same width as the gaps. Remove the burrs afterwards, by polishing.

7 Starter motor switch - function, removal and examination

1 When the handlebar starter button is depressed, the solenoid switch is energised, which in turn makes the circuit between the battery and starter. A solenoid switch is necessary to withstand the heavy current (approx. 100 amps) needed to produce the starting torque which would otherwise overload the handlebar switch.

2 When the starter button is pressed a click should be heard from inside the solenoid. This indicates that the contacts inside the switch are closing. If the solenoid malfunctions, first check the handlebar button is earthing. No repair is possible and if the switch is faulty, a replacement solenoid will have to be obtained.

8 Ignition and light switch

1 The ignition and lighting switch are integral and operated by a key which cannot be removed when the ignition is switched on.

2 A replacement key can be obtained if the number on it is quoted.

3 It is not practical to repair the ignition switch if it malfunctions. A new lock and matching key will have to be obtained.

9 Handlebar switches

1 If a switch malfunctions, very little can be done except by cleaning the contacts. If this is ineffective, a replacement unit will have to be obtained.

2 It is worth noting that there are several aerosol-type sprays on the market that are exceptionally good at cleaning switch contacts. Often, this will save needless dismantling once access has been gained to the contacts themselves.

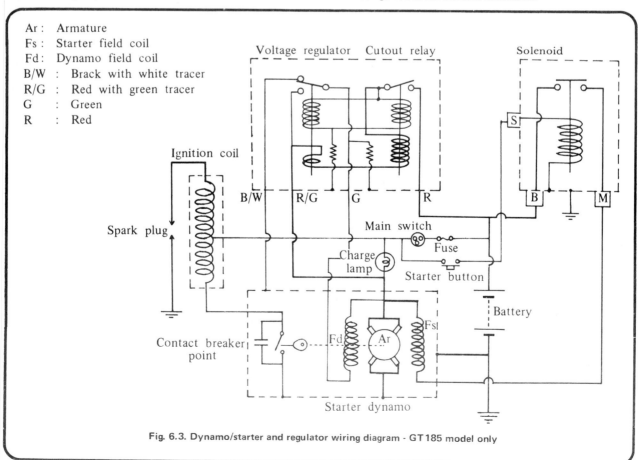

Ar : Armature
Fs : Starter field coil
Fd : Dynamo field coil
B/W : Brack with white tracer
R/G : Red with green tracer
G : Green
R : Red

Fig. 6.3. Dynamo/starter and regulator wiring diagram - GT185 model only

4.2 The rectifier is located behind the fuse bracket

5.2 This cover has to be removed to check and clean the contacts

6.5a Lift up clip and slide out bush

6.5b Check the commutator surface for scoring

10 Stop light switch - adjustment

1 The stop light switch is located below the oil tank and is operated by the brake pedal via a spring.
2 The operation of the switch should always be checked after adjusting the rear chain or rear brake since these adjustments may alter the setting.
3 The switch should be actuated when the brake pedal is depressed and the brake shoes make initial contact with the brake drum. Adjustment is achieved by screwing the two nuts down to operate the switch sooner, or up to operate it later.

11 Flasher unit - location and checking

1 The flasher unit is located underneath the tank, behind the ignition coils. When functioning normally, it will produce an audible click. If the unit appears to malfunction it can be checked as follows:
2 Connect the flasher unit as shown in Fig. 6.4. The bulb should flash continuously with a constant frequency. If it fails to operate, a new unit will have to be obtained. The usual cause of the indicators malfunctioning is a poor earth (or blown bulb) at one or more of the indicator units.

7.2 The solenoid is retained by a single bolt

11.1 The flasher unit is rubber mounted from the top frame tube

11.2 Check the earth connection on the indicators

12.1 Note the rubber rim seal

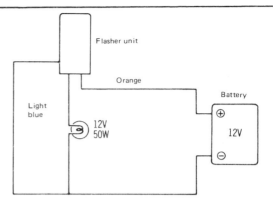

Fig. 6.4. Flasher unit testing circuit

---

12 Direction indicators - bulb and lens replacement

1   To remove the lens undo the two screws; note the rubber sealing washer behind the lens.
2   The bulb is of the bayonet type and when renewing, ensure that the correct wattage (23W) is fitted, otherwise the indicators will malfunction.
3   When replacing the lens make sure to fit the rubber gasket. Do not overtighten the screws, or the plastic lens will crack.

---

13 Headlamp - replacing bulb and beam height adjustment

1   The headlamp is retained by two screws, one on either side at the bottom of the rim. Access to the bulb is held in position by a plastic holder. The bulb is removed by twisting the holder in the reflector. The parking light (when fitted) is a push fit into the reflector.
3   The reflector can be removed from the rim by unclipping the three wire clips that hold it in position on the headlamp rim.
4   The beam height can be adjusted by slackening the two headlamp bracket bolts which hold the headlamp shell in position. This allows the beam to be adjusted up or down. Do not forget to retighten the bolts after adjustment.
5   UK lighting regulations stipulate that the lighting system must be arranged so that the light does not dazzle a person standing in the same horizontal plane as the vehicle, at a distance greater than 25 feet from the lamp, whose eye level is not less than 3 feet 6 inches above that plane. It is easy to approximate this setting by placing the machine 25 feet away from a wall, on a level road, and setting the beam height so that it is concentrated at the same height as the distance from the centre of the headlamp to the ground. The rider must be seated normally during this operation, and the pillion passenger, if one is carried regularly.

---

14 Instrument and warning lights - bulb replacement

1   All the warning light bulbs are contained in the tachometer head, along with its own illuminating light. The speedometer has only the one internal illumination bulb. To gain access to the light bulbs, either the speedometer or tachometer (which ever is appropriate) has to be removed from its bracket.
2   Unscrew the drive cable nut and pull the cable clear of the instrument head. Undo the two securing nuts. Note that anti-vibration rubbers are fitted. Lift the head clear of its brackets. The bulb holders are a push fit in the head. The bulbs are of the bayonet type and are all rated at 3.4W, with the exception of the direction indicator bulb, which is rated at 1.7W.
3   Replacement is a reversal of the above. Do not omit the rubber washers.

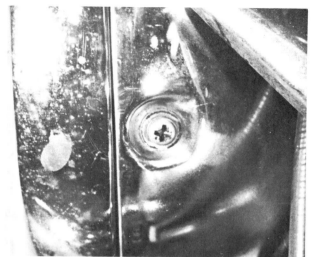

13.1a Remove both the left and ...

13.1b ... right hand screws

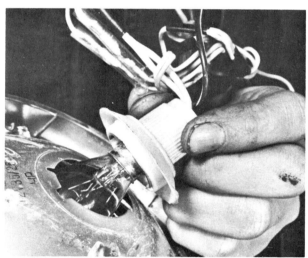

13.2a Remove the bulb holder and ...

13.2b ... detach the bulb

13.3 The reflector unit is retained by three wire clips

13.4 Slacken the headlight bolts to adjust the beam height

14.2a Unscrew the cable nut and pull the cable clear

15 Rear and stop lamp - bulb and lens replacement

1   To remove the lens undo the two screws; note the rubber sealing washer behind the lens.

2   The twin filament bulb is of the staggered bayonet type and therefore can be replaced only one way.

3   When replacing the lens make sure to fit the rubber gasket. Do not overtighten the screws, or the plastic lens will crack.

4   If the bulb constantly fails, check that it is earthed properly and also that the mudguard is not vibrating excessively (check securing bolts and washers etc).

14.2b Remove the nuts. Note the rubber washers.

15.1 Remove the lens cover

14.2c Lift off the instrument head

15.2 A staggered bayonet rear/stop light bulb is used

16 Horn - location and adjustment

1   The horn is secured by two bolts and is either rubber mounted or uses a flexible steel bracket. The rubber mounting or bracket is used to isolate the horn from high frequency vibrations. The horn is located either underneath the petrol tank or below the headlight.
2   On some models the horn can be adjusted by means of a small screw and locknut on the rear of the body. If the horn fails to work, first check its associated wiring and in particular the horn button earthing. It is statutory requirement in most countries that the machine is fitted with a horn in working order.

17 Wiring - layout and examination

1   The wiring is colour-coded and will correspond with the accompanying wiring diagrams.
2   Visual inspection will show whether any breaks or frayed outer coverings are giving rise to short circuits. Another source of trouble may be the snap connectors, particularly where the connector has not been pushed home fully in the outer casing.
3   Intermittent short circuits can sometimes be traced to a chafed wire which passes through a frame member. Avoid tight bends in the wire or situations where the wire can become trapped or stretched between casings.

18 Fault diagnosis - electrical system

Symptom	Cause	Remedy
Complete electrical failure	Blown fuse	Check wiring for loose connections before fitting new fuse
	Isolated battery	Check battery connections for signs of corrosion, remove corrosion with hot water
Constant blowing of bulbs	Vibration or poor earth connections	Check bulb holders, check earth return connections
Dim lights, horn and starter do not work	Discharged battery	Recharge battery with battery charger Check generator for output
Starter motor sluggish or will not work	Worn brushes	Remove end cover and renew brushes (GT185 model only)

Wiring diagrams, Pages 92 and 93

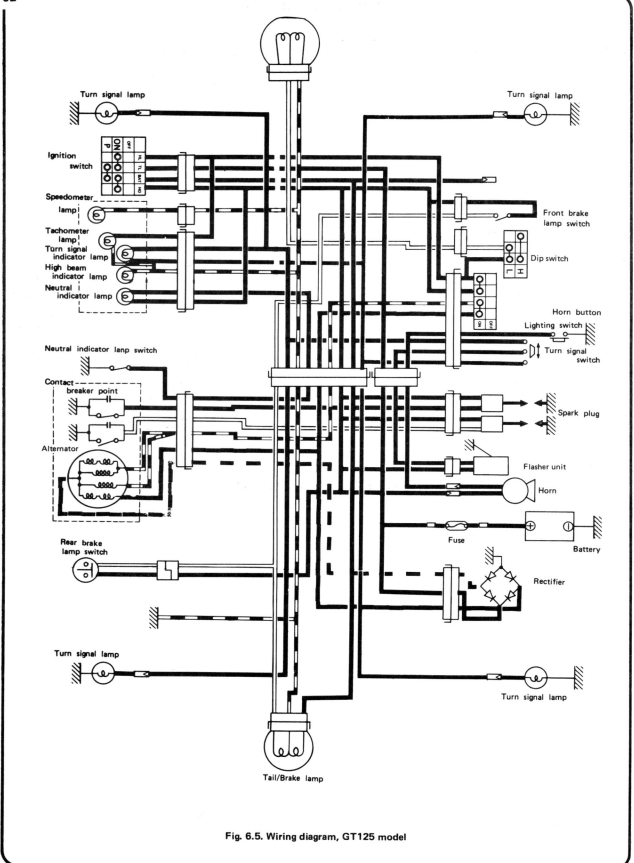

Fig. 6.5. Wiring diagram, GT125 model

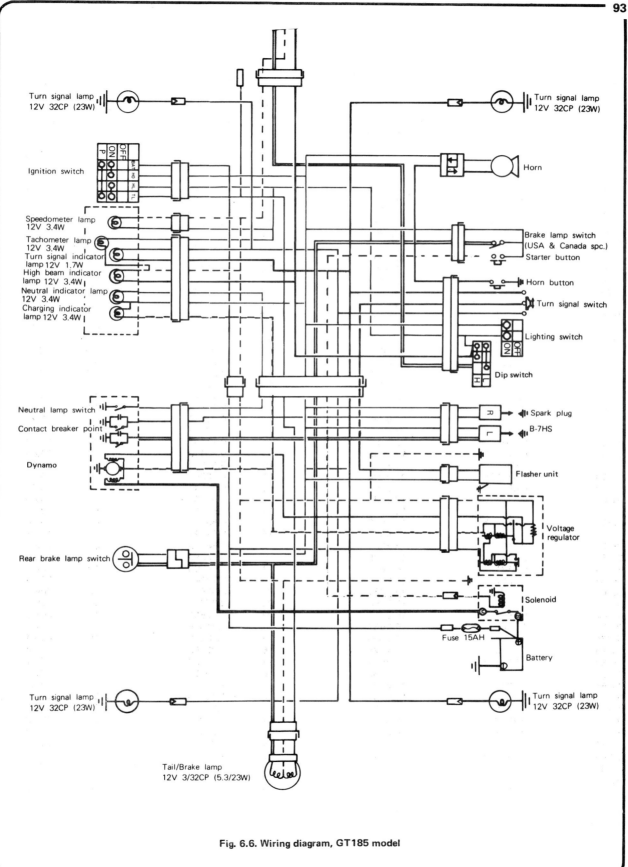

Fig. 6.6. Wiring diagram, GT185 model

Metric conversion tables

Inches	Decimals	Millimetres	Millimetres to Inches		Inches to Millimetres	
			mm	Inches	Inches	mm
1/64	0.015625	0.3969	0.01	0.00039	0.001	0.0254
1/32	0.03125	0.7937	0.02	0.00079	0.002	0.0508
3/64	0.046875	1.1906	0.03	0.00118	0.003	0.0762
1/16	0.0625	1.5875	0.04	0.00157	0.004	0.1016
5/64	0.078125	1.9844	0.05	0.00197	0.005	0.1270
3/32	0.09375	2.3812	0.06	0.00236	0.006	0.1524
7/64	0.109375	2.7781	0.07	0.00276	0.007	0.1778
1/8	0.125	3.1750	0.08	0.00315	0.008	0.2032
9/64	0.140625	3.5719	0.09	0.00354	0.009	0.2286
5/32	0.15625	3.9687	0.1	0.00394	0.01	0.254
11/64	0.171875	4.3656	0.2	0.00787	0.02	0.508
3/16	0.1875	4.7625	0.3	0.01181	0.03	0.762
13/64	0.203125	5.1594	0.4	0.01575	0.04	1.016
7/32	0.21875	5.5562	0.5	0.01969	0.05	1.270
15/64	0.234375	5.9531	0.6	0.02362	0.06	1.524
1/4	0.25	6.3500	0.7	0.02756	0.07	1.778
17/64	0.265625	6.7469	0.8	0.03150	0.08	2.032
9/32	0.28125	7.1437	0.9	0.03543	0.09	2.286
19/64	0.296875	7.5406	1	0.03937	0.1	2.54
5, 16	0.3125	7.9375	2	0.07874	0.2	5.08
21/64	0.328125	8.3344	3	0.11811	0.3	7.62
11/32	0.34375	8.7312	4	0.15748	0.4	10.16
23/64	0.359375	9.1281	5	0.19685	0.5	12.70
3/8	0.375	9.5250	6	0.23622	0.6	15.24
25/64	0.390625	9.9219	7	0.27559	0.7	17.78
13/32	0.40625	10.3187	8	0.31496	0.8	20.32
27/64	0.421875	10.7156	9	0.35433	0.9	22.86
7/16	0.4375	11.1125	10	0.39370	1	25.4
29/64	0.453125	11.5094	11	0.43307	2	50.8
15/32	0.46875	11.9062	12	0.47244	3	76.2
31/64	0.484375	12.3031	13	0.51181	4	101.6
1/2	0.5	12.7000	14	0.55118	5	127.0
33/64	0.515625	13.0969	15	0.59055	6	152.4
17/32	0.53125	13.4937	16	0.62992	7	177.8
35/64	0.546875	13.8906	17	0.66929	8	203.2
9/16	0.5625	14.2875	18	0.70866	9	228.6
37/64	0.578125	14.6844	19	0.74803	10	254.0
19/32	0.59375	15.0812	20	0.78740	11	279.4
39/64	0.609375	15.4781	21	0.82677	12	304.8
5/8	0.625	15.8750	22	0.86614	13	330.2
41/64	0.640625	16.2719	23	0.90551	14	355.6
21/32	0.65625	16.6687	24	0.94488	15	381.0
43/64	0.671875	17.0656	25	0.98425	16	406.4
11/16	0.6875	17.4625	26	1.02362	17	431.8
45/64	0.703125	17.8594	27	1.06299	18	457.2
23/32	0.71875	18.2562	28	1.10236	19	482.6
47/64	0.734375	18.6531	29	1.14173	20	508.0
3/4	0.75	19.0500	30	1.18110	21	533.4
49/64	0.765625	19.4469	31	1.22047	22	558.8
25/32	0.78125	19.8437	32	1.25984	23	584.2
51/64	0.796875	20.2406	33	1.29921	24	609.6
13/16	0.8125	20.6375	34	1.33858	25	635.0
53/64	0.828125	21.0344	35	1.37795	26	660.4
27/32	0.84375	21.4312	36	1.41732	27	685.8
55/64	0.859375	21.8281	37	1.4567	28	711.2
7/8	0.875	22.2250	38	1.4961	29	736.6
57/64	0.890625	22.6219	39	1.5354	30	762.0
29/32	0.90625	23.0187	40	1.5748	31	787.4
59/64	0.921875	23.4156	41	1.6142	32	812.8
15/16	0.9375	23.8125	42	1.6535	33	838.2
61/64	0.953125	24.2094	43	1.6929	34	863.6
31/32	0.96875	24.6062	44	1.7323	35	889.0
63/64	0.984375	25.0031	45	1.7717	36	914.4

1   Imperial gallon = 8 Imp pints = 1.16 US gallons = 277.42 cu in = 4.5459 litres

1   US gallon = 4 US quarts = 0.862 Imp gallon = 231 cu in = 3.785 litres

1   Litre = 0.2199 Imp gallon = 0.2642 US gallon = 61.0253 cu in = 1000 cc

Miles to Kilometres		Kilometres to Miles	
1	1.61	1	0.62
2	3.22	2	1.24
3	4.83	3	1.86
4	6.44	4	2.49
5	8.05	5	3.11
6	9.66	6	3.73
7	11.27	7	4.35
8	12.88	8	4.97
9	14.48	9	5.59
10	16.09	10	6.21
20	32.19	20	12.43
30	48.28	30	18.64
40	64.37	40	24.85
50	80.47	50	31.07
60	96.56	60	37.28
70	112.65	70	43.50
80	128.75	80	49.71
90	144.84	90	55.92
100	160.93	100	62.14

lb f ft to Kg f m		Kg f m to lb f ft		lb f/in^2: Kg f/cm^2		Kg f/cm^2: lb f/in^2	
1	0.138	1	7.233	1	0.07	1	14.22
2	0.276	2	14.466	2	0.14	2	28.50
3	0.414	3	21.699	3	0.21	3	42.67
4	0.553	4	28.932	4	0.28	4	56.89
5	0.691	5	36.165	5	0.35	5	71.12
6	0.829	6	43.398	6	0.42	6	85.34
7	0.967	7	50.631	7	0.49	7	99.56
8	1.106	8	57.864	8	0.56	8	113.79
9	1.244	9	65.097	9	0.63	9	128.00
10	1.382	10	72.330	10	0.70	10	142.23
20	2.765	20	144.660	20	1.41	20	284.47
30	4.147	30	216.990	30	2.11	30	426.70

Index

Printed by
J. H. HAYNES & Co. Ltd
Sparkford Yeovil Somerset
ENGLAND